WOMAN
IN THE SHADE
OF ISLAM

Prepared By:
Abdul Rahman Al-Sheha

Rendered Into English By:
DR. Mohammed Said Dabas

Introduced By:

DR. Ahmad Ibn Saifuddin

Revised By:

Abdulaziz Addwesh

Riyadh - 1421 H. = 2000 G.
Printed on the expense of
Sister Umm Amr
(May Allah forgive her and her parent)
3rd Eddition

(C) Abdul rahman bin Abdul Karim Al- Sheha 1418

King Fahd National Libarary Cataloging - in Publication Data

Abdul rahman bin . A . Al- Sheha

Women in the shade of Islam
144 P .   14 x 21 cm
ISBN : 9960 - 800 - 23 - 7

1- Women in Islam
2- Title
219, 1 dc   226/18

Legal Deposit no 226/18
ISBN : 9960 - 800 - 23 - 7

In the Name of Allah, the Most Beneficent, Most Merciful.

And when it is said to them. "Come to what Allah has revealed and to the Messenger (Muhammad ﷺ for the verdict of that which you have made unlawful)" they say: "Enough for us is that which we found our fathers following." Even though their fathers had no knowledge whatsoever nor guidance.

(AL-Maidah: 104)

Who has only turned the page, not read the book in real.

يتناول هذا الكتاب ما يأتي :

- **الأمور التي ساوى الإسلام فيها بين الرجل والمرأة :**

– المساواة في الأحكام والتكاليف الشرعية – المساواة في الثواب والعقاب الدنيوي والأخروي – المساواة في الإنسانية – المساواة في النسبة وحرية التصرفات المالية – المساواة في حفظ العرض والكرامة – المساواة في وجوب التعلم – المساواة في تحمل المسؤولية نحو إصلاح المجتمع .

- ## وضع المرأة في المجتمعات عبر العصور :

وضع المرأة في المجتمع الهندي القديم – وضع المرأة في المجتمع الجاهلي – وضع المرأة في المجتمع اليوناني القديم – وضع المرأة في المجتمع الروماني – وضع المرأة في المجتمع الصيني القديم – وضع المرأة في المجتمع اليهودي القديم – وضع المرأة في المجتمع المسيحي .

وضع المرأة وحقوقها في المجتمع الإسلامي :

–حقوق المرأة في الإسلام بنتاً – حقوق المرأة في الإسلام زوجةً – حقوق المرأة في الإسلام أمّاً – حقوقها في الإسلام كامرأة .

- ## شبهات حول حقوق المرأة في الإسلام والرد عليها :

تعدد الزوجات – المرأة والشهادة – المرأة و القوامة – المرأة والميراث – المرأة والدية – عمل المرأة – المرأة والطلاق –سفر المرأة – ضرب المرأة .

INTRODUCTION

All praise is due to Allah. May Allah's peace and blessings be upon His messenger Muhammad, his companions, his family and his followers until the day resurrection.

I am very happy to introduce this book (Women in the Shade of Islam) to all readers (Muslims and non-Muslims). The subject is very critical and the time for it is overdue.

For a long time there has been a misunderstanding of the status of women in any religion in general and Islam in particular. Throughout the ages, many nations and cultures have placed women in the lowest position against men. Men have dominated their lives and properties. This included the Arabian culture before Islam known as the Age of Ignorance. In the Greek culture, for example, women were looked at as an item in the house. She was subject to buying and selling in the market. She was deprived from the right of inheritance and was thought of as filth and a product from the deeds of the Satan. In the Roman society, the woman used to suffer all worst punishments by men such as burning her body with hot oil, tying her to posts and polling her behind speeding horses. All of this took place for no other reason other than being a woman. According to the English law, up until 1805 men could sell their wives as they would with any property!

In Islam, however, women are respected as partners of men. Their role in life is complimentary rather than contradictory. The woman in Islam has all rights of property ownership, business dealings and choosing her husband. In facing responsibilities and earning rights she is perfectly as equal as man. Men have even bigger responsibilities in carrying the burdens of earning for the family and supporting spouses. Protecting their chastity and reputation honors women. Unfortunately, many a times, the

Western culture has been degrading the status of women into the level of mere commodities.

To write a book on this subject is very much needed, and I am very much happy to present it to the readers for two reasons: the first is that I know brother Abd al-Raman al-Shiha for a period of time. I have dealt with him and found him to be one of the finest people I have met. By the grace of Allah, he has a good character and he -as I know it- is dedicated to the cause of serving Allah. Allah alone knows the best. The second is that I find this book to be interesting and beneficial. The reader, whether being a Muslim or not, will find a logical orderly and supported with evidence presentation. I also find this book to be easy to read while containing all the necessary information on such diverse and comprehensive theme.

For a serious reader this book is a must, so that s/he will know to what extent women are respected and protected in perfected Islam.

I pray that Allah would reward my brother Abd al- Raman al-Shiha for writing this book and for all his effort in the cause of serving Islam, Muslims and humanity. All praise is due to Allah the almighty.

Dr. Ahmad Ibn Saifuddin

Institute of Islamic and Arabic Sciences in America

Translator's Word

Dear Reader,

I would like to share with you few things I learned while translating this booklet. It is, I believe, only fair and just to note here that although there are quite a number of books about *WOMEN* in Islam that tackle rights, education, inheritance and other topics, I strongly feel that this book has introduced a comprehensive and exhaustive account of all these topics put together.

The booklet gives accurate historical, social and political accounts of *WOMEN* from an Islamic perspective. All these ideas are supported with valid quotations from various resources.

In a nut shell, the book is a good start for a person, male and female alike, who is interested in learning the view point of Islam on *WOMEN* and wants to keep this in perspective and comparative with other religions and societies.

This work, I believe, is a courageous attempt to present the Islamic views about *WOMEN* in a simple, yet friendly atmosphere.

I do hope that the reader will benefit from this humble contribution. Any comments, objections and corrections on the translation and editing are welcome. Please contact the translator at:

P.O. Box 25283, Riyadh, Kingdom of Saudi Arabia 11466, Fax: (+009661) 465-2597 Your contributions are appreciated and valued.

Appreciation

The translator wishes to express his deep appreciation, gratitude and warmest thanks to Mr. Hadi Abughazalah, and Mrs. Kawther M. Hall, who, both, have greatly contributed to the polishing, editing, formatting, revision and moral and mental support while rendering this book into English.

This rendering, I have to admit, was not possible without their relentless efforts, sincere work to present the book in the best possible fashion. Together we worked as one team whose essential aim was to produce a useful and accurate piece of literature that is of benefit to those who are interested in learning about the view point of Islam on this subject.

I am truly indebted to both of them. I can neither thank them enough, nor reward them for what they have done, but I pray Allah, (ﷻ) to bless them for their efforts and reward them according to His Generosity.

Mohammed Said Dabas,
The Translator
Riyadh, Kingdom of Saudi Arabia 1997

Introduction

All praise is due to Allah (ﷻ). May Allah's peace and blessings be upon His final Prophet and Messenger to mankind, Mohammad bin Abdillah. May Allah's blessings be upon all the rightly guided companions, and household of Allah's Prophet (ﷺ).

I believe I will not present any new issues or items on the topic, "Women's Rights in Islam". However, I have attempted to collect, arrange and summarize all I could find of the writings on this subject and present it in a new fashion for the benefit of the reader.

I hope, seek and pray for guidance from Allah (ﷻ), in this regard. I also hope to be successful in reaching my goals. Allah (ﷻ), stated in the Glorious Quran 49:13 which the meaning of is translated as:

"O Mankind! We have created you from a male and a female, and made you into nations and tribes, that you may know one another. Verily, the most honorable of you in the Sight of Allah is the believer who has Taqwa (i.e. piety and righteousness) and loves Allah most. Verily, Allah is All-Knowing, All-Aware."

Mr. Ghalayenee, the author of *Islam Is the Spirit of Civilization*, (in Arabic), stated on page 267, quoting from *"The Crescent and the Cross"*, quoting the well known French thinker and philosopher, Voltaire, in his book *The Dictionary of Philosophy*, under the essay "The Quran":

"We have attributed many ridiculous things to the Quran of which it is indeed pure. Our authors, who increased in numbers, notably find it easy to rally women behind their party by convincing them that Mohammad (ﷺ) considered them merely intelligent animals. Further, women are, in the sight of Islamic Laws, no more than owned slaves who own nothing of their world, and are entitled to nothing in the hereafter either."

It is very obvious that statements as such are nothing but falsehood. Yet, there were readers who believed such statements.

We do not ignore the fact that the Quran has given men a special natural characteristic. The Quran, however, differs from the Old Testament which considers the weakness of the woman a divine punishment, as it was stated in Genesis 3:16 which the meaning of is translated as:

"Unto the woman he said, I will greatly multiply thy sorrow and thy conception; in sorrow thou shalt bring forth children; and thy desire shall be to thy husband, and he shall rule over thee."

It is a great confusion to attribute to a great legislator like Mohammad, such unacceptable treatment of women. The truth is that the Quran stated 4:19 which the meaning of is translated as:

"...If you dislike them, it may be that you dislike one thing and Allah brings through it a great deal of good."

Also, in verse 30:21 which the meaning of is translated as:

"And among His Signs is this, that He created for you wives from among yourselves, that you may find repose in them, and He has put between you affection and mercy. Verily, in that are indeed signs for people who reflect."

Abdul Rahman bin Abdul Karim Al-Sheha

E.mail. **alsheha@cocg.org**

www.Islamland.org

K.S.A RIYADH 11535 P.O.BOX (59565)

Chapter One

Slogans

It has been recorded in recent history that many calls have been made for women's rights. Calls for women's freedom, liberation and equal rights with men have been heard all over the world. Such calls are acceptable in societies and countries where women are neither given their due rights, nor are being fairly and justly treated.

It is stunning and surprising, however, to hear such calls in Islamic societies where women have been fairly treated and were given their rights more than fourteen hundred years ago, and without any calls made by them, or rather by their advocates.

Close examination of the slogans announced and called for by the women's liberation movement shows that they hinge on the following three elements:

- Calling for women's liberation
- Calling for women's equal rights with men
- Demanding for women's rights

Calling for Women's Liberation

The word "liberation" indicates, first, that there are certain shackles, limitations, and bonds, restrictions or chains in place. Thus, we believe that there are many fallacies or distortions in using the term "women's liberation." The term "women's liberation" indicates that women are enslaved, and they must be liberated; that is not the case, indeed.

Absolute liberty is, rather, impossible. Man is naturally restricted and has many limitations due to his limited abilities and capabilities. Man, in general, in any given society, primitive or civilized, lives under certain laws, rules and regulations that normally govern his life and organize all various affairs of life. Does that mean, by any standard, that man is not sovereign, independent or free?

Freedom or liberty has, therefore, certain limits which, if exceeded, will lead to uncivilized activities which do not abide by any laws, rules, regulations or standards. Islam is the first law, or system of living, which granted women freedom and liberation. It granted women the right to deal with the society directly, rather than dealing via a guardian who is officially responsible and in charge of running all the woman's affairs (economically, socially, politically and otherwise).

Islam has forbidden women from being publicly indecent, sexually provocative and acting as a sex agent, subject or any similar form. This is a freedom from which the male in Islam, equally, as well, has been stripped.

Allah's Prophet (ﷺ) clearly stated:

"The example of a person who keeps the restricted and imposed laws, restrictions and commands of Allah (ﷻ), and the person who breaks them are examples of two groups of people who were in a ship and decided to divide it amongst them equally. One group got the upper deck as their lot, while the other group got the lower part of the ship. Whenever the people in the lower part of the ship need to get water they had to pass through the

territory of the people on the upper deck (thus imposing on them and bothering them with their passage). The people in the lower part thought to themselves 'If we drill a hole in our portion of the ship, we can have access to the water without disturbing the party on the upper deck.' If the group on the upper deck let the group on the lower part of the ship does what they thought was right (drill a hole in the lower part of the ship to gain access to water), all the people on the ship would be destroyed. However, if they forbid them from doing so, they would all be safe."[1]

In fact, Islam illustrates the concept of freedom and liberty in such a way that individual behavior and conduct must not, by any means, be either harmful to the individual himself or destructive to the society at large.

A well-known German thinker and philosopher, Schopenhauer said:

"Grant woman total and absolute freedom and liberty for ONE YEAR ONLY, and check with me after that to see the results of such freedom. Do not forget that you (all), along with me will inherit virtues, chastity and good morals. If I die (before then) you are free to say either: "He was wrong!" or "He hit the heart of the truth!"[2]

It is suitable to record here the confession by an American female reporter who is syndicated in over 250 newspapers, worked in the area of journalism and broadcasting for over 20 years, and

---

[1] This Hadith is reported by Imam Bukhari.

[2] Ghalayenee, *A Word about Women*, he quoted from Schopenhauer book *Islam, the Spirit of Civilization*, page 224.

who has visited numerous Islamic countries, Helesian Stansbery. She said at the end of one of her visits to an Islamic country: *"The Arab-Islamic society is wholesome and healthy. This society must continue to protect its traditions that restrict both its males and females to a certain and reasonable degree. This society definitely differs from the European and American societies. The Arab-Islamic society has its own traditions that impose certain restrictions and limitations on women, respect and obedience to parents, and imposes most restrictions. First and foremost, the most strict restrictions and limitations are on absolute sexual freedom that truly threatens both the society and the family in Europe and the United States of America. Therefore, the restrictions that are imposed by the Arab-Islamic society are valid and beneficial as well. I strongly recommend that you adhere to your traditions and code of ethics. Forbid coeducation. Restrict female freedom, or rather, return back to the full 'purdah' practices. Truly this is better for you than the sexual freedom of Europe and the United States of America. Forbid coeducation because we have suffered from it in the USA. The American society has become sophisticated, full of all forms and terms of sexual freedom. The victims of sexual freedom and coeducation are filling the prisons, sidewalks, bars, taverns and whore houses. The (false) freedom that we have granted to our young females and daughters has turned them to drugs, crime and white slavery. Coeducation, sexual freedom and all other types of "freedom" in the European and American societies have threatened the family and shaken moral values and ethics."*[3]

---

[3] Abdullah bin Wokayil Al-Shaikh, in his book *The Woman and the Enemies' Plot.*

The question that poses itself here to the women's liberation advocates is: "What is the best, most beneficial and more protecting system for the honor, dignity and pride of women?"

Woman's Equality with Men

Woman's equality with men is impossibility. The very nature of men and women is different in terms of physical, mental and psychological abilities.

If equality between all members of the same gender is impossible, regardless whether the gender is masculine or feminine, due to natural differences, it is impossible to be equal between two genders. This is only natural. Allah Almighty, stated in the Glorious Quran 51:49 which the meaning of is translated as:

"And of everything We have created pairs, that you may remember (the Grace of Allah)."

Truly, Islam treats women with fairness and justice and preserves and protects all the rights, to which she is entitled, as we shall illustrate throughout this book.

  1. Islam requires equal religious duties, requirements and rituals of the woman, as required of man. Prayer (Salah), fasting (Sawm), charity (Zakah) and pilgrimage (Hajj) are equally required of both genders. Islam, however, considers woman in some cases by making the requirements a little lighter on her in terms of religious rules and regulations, such as dropping both the prayers and the fasting of a menstruating woman or a woman in the state of after-birth confinement. A woman is required, however to make up the days of fasting she has missed due to menses. This has been imposed in such a way only to take the woman's health and physical situation into consideration during menses and confinement periods.

"From the very beginning of creation, male has been distinguished and differentiated from female. Still, one completes the other. Based upon this, we believe such a precise division in terms of the sexes does entail two different missions in life, otherwise, there would be no need for such differences in the sexes. Moreover, this indicates that each sex has its own merits, while both are human beings. We can easily recognize the difference between day and night, although both help us realize one thing, "TIME". The daytime grants us the ability to seek our daily provision, while the night grants us the peace to rest. Man and woman, in this aspect of required from men ONLY, based on his sex. Similarly, there are certain things that are required from the woman ONLY, based on her natural preparation. Yet, both man and woman are human beings who share many common characteristics. "[4]

Allah Almighty, stated in the Glorious Quran 9:71 which the meaning of is translated as:

---

[4] Shaikh Mitwalli Al-Shi'rawee, in his book *Fate and Predestiny*

"The believers, men and women, are helpers, supporters, friends and protectors of one another. They enjoin all that is good, and forbid (people) from all what is evil, they offer their prayers perfectly, and give the Zakah and obey Allah and His Messenger. Allah will bestow Mercy on them. Surely Allah is All-Mighty, All-Wise."

2. Islam has entitled both males and females to the same worldly and Hereafter reward and penalty. They both are equal in terms of reward and punishment as stated in Glorious Quran 16:97 which the meaning of is translated as:

"Whoever does righteous acts, whether male or female, while he (or she) is a true believer (of Islamic Monotheism) verily, to him We will give a good life (in this world with respect, contentment and lawful provisions), and We shall pay them certainly a reward in proportion to the best of what they are used to (i.e. Paradise in the Hereafter)."

3. Islam made both the male and the female equal in terms of humanity. Islam does not categorize woman as the source of *"Original Sin"* that caused Adam (ﷺ) to be dismissed from Jannah (paradise), as other religious teaching dictate. Allah Almighty, stated in the Glorious Quran 4:1 which the meaning of is translated as:

"O mankind! Be dutiful to your Lord, Who created you from a single person (Adam), and from him (Adam) He created his wife (Eve), and from them both He created many men and women..."

Allah (ﷻ) stated in the Glorious Quran 75:36-39 which the meaning of is translated as:

"Does man think that he will be left neglected without being punished or rewarded for the obligatory duties enjoined by his Lord (Allah) on him? Was he not a mixed male and female discharge of semen pouring forth? Then he became a clot; then (Allah) shaped and fashioned (him) in due proportion, and made him into two sexes, male and female."

Allah illustrated in the quoted verses from Glorious Quran that He created both sexes from one single source. There is no difference in creation between both sexes. There is no difference between both sexes in terms of qualifications as well. Both are very much alike. Thus, Islam canceled and abrogated all previous unfair and unjust laws and systems against women, especially those which considered women of inferior quality or nature to that of men. Consequently, due to these misconceptions, women have been deprived of many of their human rights. Allah's Prophet (ﷺ) said, as reported by Tirmithee:

"Women are but (equal) brethren for men.

4. 'Islam has entitled women to the same rights insofar as chastity, integrity and personal honor and respect are concerned. Any person who falsely accuses any chaisty woman with adultry or fornication shall be publicly punished, similar to the

treatment of man. Allah (ﷻ), stated in the Glorious Quran 24:4 which the meaning of is translated as:

"And those who accuse chaste women, and produce not four witnesses, flog them with eighty lashes, and reject their testimony forever, they indeed are the liars, rebellious and disobedient to Allah."

5. Islam considers women equally qualified insofar as financial dealings are concerned. Woman, according to Islamic rules, regulations and teachings, can own, buy, sell and undertake any type of financial transaction without the need for guardianship, restrictions or limitations.

6. Islam indicated that whosoever honors, respects and deals with women with integrity and respect possesses an integral, healthy and fully composed personality. On the other hand, a man who mistreats women, insults them, humiliates them or subjects them to unnecessary humiliation is a mean, dishonest and disrespected man. Allah's Prophet (ﷺ) is reported to have said:
"Only an honorable man treats women with honor and integrity. And only a mean, deceitful and dishonest man humiliates and insults women."⁵

---

⁵ This Hadith is reported by Ibn 'Asaker.

7. Islam entitles women to the same rights in terms of education. Allah's Prophet (ﷺ) said, as reported by Baihaqee,

"Seeking knowledge is compulsory for each and every Muslim (i.e., male and female)."

Muslim scholars collectively agreed that the word *"Muslim"* includes both male and female, as we indicated between brackets. Similarly, Islam entitles women to the same equal right to raise children in the best form, shape and format in accordance with right Islamic guidance and means of education. Allah's Prophet (ﷺ) is reported to have said,

"He whosoever has a daughter and he does not bury her alive, humiliate [insult or degrade] her and does not give preference to his son over her, such a person will be granted entry to Paradise by Allah."[6]

8. Islam places woman in an equal position to that of men in terms of the responsibility of reforming the society in general. , male and female, man and woman, equally shoulder the responsibility of enjoining good and forbidding evil in society. Allah (ﷻ), stated in the Glorious Quran 9:71 which the meaning of is translated as:

"The believers, men and women, are helpers, supporters, friends and protectors of one another, they enjoin all that is

---

[6] Reported by al-Hakim and al-Naisaburi.

good, and forbid all that is evil, they offer their prayers perfectly, and give Zakah and obey Allah and His Messenger. Allah will bestow Mercy on them. Surely Allah is All-Mighty, All-Wise."

Demanding Women's Rights

The core of our discussion in this book is the demanding of women's rights. We would like to point out at the very beginning that there is not a single law, system or regulation that preserves, maintains and protects woman's rights as much as Islam does, whether in the past or in modern times. And this shall be noted in the following discussions throughout this book.

It is sufficient, we believe, to quote non-Muslim scholars' statements in this regard;

Sir Hamilton, the well-known English thinker and philosopher stated in his book *Islam and Arab Civilization,*

"The rules, regulations and verdicts concerning women in Islam are clear, frank and open. Islam capitalizes on the complete care that should be given to the protection of woman against anything that may harm her personally, or causes ill-fame, reputation or character."

Gustave Le Bond, the well-known French thinker stated in his book *The Arab Civilization* (p.488),

"Islamic virtuous deeds are not limited to honoring and respecting women, but rather, we can add that Islam is the first

*religion to honor and respect.   We can easily prove this by
illustrating that all religions and nations, prior to the advent of
Islam, caused much harm and insult to women."*

He also pointed out (p.497),

*"Matrimonial rights which have   been stated and illustrated in
the Glorious Quran and by the interpreters of the meanings of
the Glorious Quran are far better than European matrimonial
rights for both husband and wife."*

Over fourteen hundred years   ago, Islam began to spread in the
known world following the commission of Allah's Prophet (ﷺ)
Mohammad bin Abdillah, of Makkah. , spread its light through
the teachings that   came with the Glorious Quran, and the
traditions of Allah's Prophet (ﷺ). The Islamic teachings made a
great impact, change   and influence on the lives of the followers
of Islam as a religion and a way of life. Consequently, these
changes affected the entire societies in which Muslims lived,
traveled and settled. The advent of Islam was   different in all
aspects. It spread very rapidly in the known world, and was
known,   and still is, as the most comprehensive life system. Islam
is found to be exact, accurate and explicit in every point. It
addresses every human need,   and does not contradict, clash or
reject any lawful,   sound and meaningful requirements of human
being's very existence which are essential to his continuity in life.

We would like to focus here on the changes that Islam brought in
terms of woman and her rights, with which we are concerned in
this book. It is suggested, therefore, that in order to have a

complete, thorough and clear picture about this subject one must examine, study and explore the status of women prior to the advent of Islam and further, compare these facts with the changes that occurred after the application of Islam in the lives of people in the Islamic society.

Chapter Two

Status of Women throughout Ages

Women in the Pre-Islamic Society

Prior to the commission of Allah's Messenger (ﷺ) as a Prophet and Messenger, women suffered great injustice, unfair treatment and were exposed to humiliation of all kinds. Women were not entitled to inherit from their parents, husband or other relatives because Arabs believed inheritance should only be granted to those who could ride a horse, fight, gain war booties and help protect the tribe and territory. In fact, more humiliation was even applied to women, in that she herself could be inherited as a commodity after the death of her indebted husband. Women were treated like material items of this world. If a woman's deceased husband had adult sons from other marriages, the oldest son amongst them had the right to add the wife of his deceased father to his household, exactly as such a son inherits the wealth of his deceased father. This widow, the wife of the deceased, was unable to leave the house of her stepson unless she paid a ransom for her life and liberation.

Women, also were forbidden to remarry if a husband divorced them. Women had no right then to choose, or even consent, to their marriage. Man, on the other hand, had the freedom to acquire as many wives as so desired, with no set limit. Moreover, there was no justice system that may forbid a man from practicing anything unjust or unfair to his wives.

Arabs, during the pre-Islamic era, never liked or welcomed the birth of a female baby into their family. They hated such a birth, and considered it an evil and bad omen. A father who received the news of the birth of a female baby was usually extremely sad, disappointed and depressed. Allah (﷿), described the father's situation when receiving the news about the birth of a daughter in the family in the pre-Islamic era:

"When the news of (the birth of) a female (baby) is brought to any of them, his face becomes dark, and he is filled with inward grief! He hides himself from the people because of the evil of that whereof he has been informed. Shall he keep her with dishonor or bury her in the Earth? Certainly, evil is their decision." [7]

Women even were not able to practice some natural rights, such as eating certain types of foods for instance. Some specific types of food were allowed only for males. Allah (﷿), stated in the Glorious Quran 6:139 which the meaning of is translated as:

"And they say: 'What is in the bellies of such cattle (milk or fetus) is for the male alone, and forbidden from our females (girls and women), however, if it was born dead, then all have shares therein..."

In fact, the hatred of female baby girls reached the extent of burying them alive at a very early age. Some Arab tribes were well known for burying their newborn girls alive at a very early age. The reasons for burial of young females alive varied,

---

[7] Glorious Quran 16:58-59.

however, according to the social status of the family. Some families, or rather the head of the family, the father, buried their daughters at a very early age fearing a shame that girls may bring to the family (if they are indulged in any shameful practices, i.e. adultery, fornication or prostitution). Allah (ﷻ), stated in the Glorious Quran 81:8-9 with reference to the Day of Judgment which the meaning of is translated as:

"And when the female (infant) buried alive [as the pagan Arabs used to do] shall be questioned; for what sin she was killed?"

Other fathers used to bury alive their female child at a very early age if the child was leprous, lame or had any other major handicap or birth defect. Those were the poor Arab pagans. Allah (ﷻ), stated in the Glorious Quran 17:31 which the meaning of is translated as,

"And kill not your children for fear of poverty. We provide for them and you. Surely, the killing of them is a great sin."

The only thing women could be proud of during the pre-Islamic era was the protection of the man and his revenge against others who humiliate or dishonor her in an attempt to maintain her dignity and honor in the tribe.

Women in the Indian Society

Women were treated as maids or slave-girls in the Indian society. Women had no will or desire of their [8]own. They followed their husbands fully with no questions asked. Women were easily lost in a gambling game played by the husband[9]. They were never allowed to remarry after the death of their husbands. In fact, women were not even entitled to live after the death of their husbands as both usually were burned in the same funeral pyre[10]. The widow had to be buried on the same day of the death of her husband.[11]

This practice lasted until the end of the 17th century when this custom was outlawed in spite of the dismay caused to the Hindu religious leaders. In fact, in certain areas of India, women were brought as a sacrifice to the Hindu gods in order to please them or to seek the fall of rain from heaven. Some Hindu laws declare that;

---

[8] See *Pre-Islamic Religious Books,* Pages 168-169, by Ali Abdulwahid Wafi. See further *Woman In Islam and International Laws,* Page 14, by Salim Bahnasi, Dar al-Kalam, Kuwait, 1986.

[9] *What Has the World Lost in Muslim Degeneration,* Pages 60-61, by Nadawi, quoting "the Great Indian Battle" of the story of Baharat.

[10] *The Story of Civilization,* Voluntary.3, pages 178, 180, 181, by W. Durant. Translated by: Mohammed Badran.

[11] See *Comparative Religions,* Part-3, Page 208 by Dr Ahmad Shalabi. See also Arab civilization by G. Lebon Pages 406-408, translated by Zuaiter. You may further refer to *The Story of Civilization,* Part-3, Pages 177-178 and 180-181 by W. Durant, translation of Muhammad Badran.

"The predestined patience, the blowing wind or tornadoes, death, hellfire, poison, snakes and fire are no less worse than women (the female)."[12]

It is also stated in Hindu religious books,[13] that "When Manna (the Hindu god of creation) created women he imposed onto them the love of bed, seats, decoration [make-up], filthy lust (of all types and kinds), anger, rebellion against honor and dignity and evil attitude, behavior and conduct."[14] In the teachings of Manna Herma Sistra[15] concerning women, one can read:

"A woman may live without any choice regardless of whether she is a little girl, a young lady or a mature woman. A young girl is under the command and choice of her father. A married woman is under the command and choice of her husband. A widow is under the command and choice of her male children, and she may never become independent (after the death of her husband). A widow may never remarry after the death of her husband, but rather she must neglect all that she likes in terms of food, clothes, and makeup until she dies. A woman may not actually own, or possess anything, as whatever she may gain or

---

[12] Dr. Mostafa Al-Siba'iee, in his book *"Woman between Jurisprudence and Law"*.

[13] Manna is a very strange personality, which has been surrounded with a lot of mystery in the Hindus culture. Some classify Manna as a god above people while other Hindu books classify him as the grandfather of their people.

[14] Ahmad Abdul Azeez Al-Hosaiyin *Woman and her Position in Islam*.

[15] Abbas Mahmoud Al-'Akkad, *Woman in the Glorious Quran*.

acquire shall go straight and immediately to the ownership of her husband."[16]

In fact, in some, maybe rare cases a woman may have several husbands at the same time[17]. This made her look like a prostitute in the society.

Women in the Chinese Society

Women in the Chinese society occupied a very low place. She used to be assigned the most despised and least important jobs and positions. The male child, however, was treated and looked upon as a *"gift"* from God. As for the female child, nobody cared for her, but rather they would be pleased to see her die. A Chinese proverb says: *'Listen to your wife, but never believe what she says."*[18] Therefore, we notice that the status of women in the Chinese society was not much better than that of the pagan Arab pre-Islamic society.

---

[16] See *Women In Islam* page 183 by Dr Samia Munaisi, quoting the last report of the International Seminar on Illiteracy on 1 December 1990, by UNESCO, entitled *Islam and Woman Education* by Nakib Exor Nicole Page 44 (ED/91/WS/22).

[17] *What Has the World Lost in Muslim Degeneration*, Pages 60-61, By Nadawi, quoting R.C.Dutt. 331.

[18] See *Arab Civilization* Page 406 by Dr G. Lebon, Translation of Zuaiter.

Women in the Roman Society

The woman in the Roman society was looked upon as a minor who could not run her own affairs. Men directed all of women's affairs. All authorities were in the hands of men. Men enjoyed full rights over their family's affairs. Men had the authority to sentence their wives to death in certain cases in which a woman was accused with certain crimes.[19] Similarly, men, as fathers, had the authority to run their daughters-in-law's affairs (the wives of their sons and grandsons). The authority of man over woman in the Roman society included, but not limited to the following: Selling the woman, torturing her, sending her into exile or killing her. The woman in the Roman society had to listen, obey and execute fully what the man says or judges. Women were deprived of the right of inheritance. In the meanwhile, the heir of the deceased father was his eldest son. In fact, Roman society permitted the man to add to the family members any person who might not belong to that specific family. Similarly, men had the right to kick out or sell any member of the family[20]

---

[19] *The Story of Civilization*, by W. Durant, Vol. 9, pages 118, 119 and 120. Translated by Mohammed Badran.

[20] *Comparative Religions* page 188, Part 3, by Dr Ahmad Shalabi. Also, *Arab Civilization*, Page 408. Rendered into Arabic by Adel Zuaiter. Al-Halabi Press - Egypt.

Women in the Greek Society

Women in the Greek society did not enjoy any better status[21]. Women were deprived of the right to education. In fact, women were very discerned in the Greek society to the extent that man claimed that *"Women are nothing but all evil."*[22] There was no system to protect women in this society. Women were sold and bought like any other commodity. Women were deprived of the right of inheritance as well. Moreover, women in this society were considered minors who had no right to make any transaction with their own wealth. Women, throughout their lives, were subjected to the will of men. Women had no right to seek divorce. Divorce was an absolute right of man that led some Greek thinkers to say, *"Women's name must be locked up in the house, as it is the case with her body."*[23]

Women in the Greek society therefore were in the lowest position.

Gustave Le Bond, the French thinker, stated in his book *Arab Civilization:*[24]

"Greeks, in general, considered women as the lowest creatures of the low. They were useful for nothing other than reproduction

---

[21] *Arab Civilization*, by Dr. G. Lebon, translated by Zuaiter, page 408.

[22] *Ibid.*, page 208, Part 3.

[23] *The Story of Civilization*, by W. Durant, Vol. 7, pages 117 and 118. Translated by Mohammed Badran.

[24] *Arab Civilization*, Page 406. Rendered into Arabic by Adel Zuaiter. Al-Halabi Press - Egypt.

and taking care of the household affairs. If a woman gave birth to an 'ugly, retarded or handicapped' child, the man could take the liberty to kill the (unwanted or undesirable) child."

Demosthenes, the well-known Greek speaker and thinker even said:

"We, Greek men, enjoyed the company of prostitutes for sexual pleasure, 'girl-friends', sweet-hearts, to care for our daily needs and we marry to get 'legitimate' children."[25]

So, we can see what fortune women had in such a society based on the statement issued by one of their best and well-known thinkers!

Women in the Old Jewish Society

Women in the old Jewish society were not more fortunate than those previously described. In the Old Testament 7:25-26 women were described as follows:

"Both my heart and I searched and sought wisdom and good judgment, to know that evil (acts) are nothing but ignorance, and stupidity, foolishness and madness. I found that more better than death is a woman as she is a net, her heart is a trap, and her hands are shackles (or handcuffs)."[26]

---

[25] Husain Al-Shaikh, *Studies in the Greek and Romans Civilization.* Page 149.

[26] Shawqee Abu-Khaleel, *Islam in the Accusation Cage.*

In the book of Exodus 21:7-11:

"7. And if a man sells his daughter to be a maidservant, she shall not go out as the menservants do. 8. If she pleases not her master, who has betrothed her to himself, then shall he let her be redeemed: to sell her unto a strange nation he shall have no power, seeing he has dealt deceitfully with her. 9. And if he had betrothed her unto his son, he shall deal with her after the manner of daughters. 10. If he take him another wife, her food, her raiment, and her duty of marriage, shall he not diminish. 11. If he does not do these three unto her, then shall she go out free without money."

Thus, if a Jewish woman got married, her guardianship was transferred from her father to her husband and she became as one of his possessions such as his house, his slave, his maidservant or his money or wealth.

This is also understood from Exodus 20:17:

"Thou shalt not covet thy neighbor's house, thou shalt not covet thy neighbor's wife, nor his manservant, nor his ox, nor his ass, nor anything that is thy neighbor's."

In addition, the Jewish teachings and laws deprived the girl from her father's inheritance if the father had other male children. In the Old Testament, the book of Numbers 27:8:

"And thou shalt speak unto the children of Israel 'If a man dies, and has no son, then ye shall cause his inheritance to pass unto his daughters'."

Moreover, Jewish men never slept in the same bed with a menstruating woman, eat with her or drink with her. Jewish men used to isolate themselves fully from a menstruating woman until she is completely free from menses.

Women in the Old Christian Society

Christian priests went to the extreme considering the woman as the cause of "original sin" and the source of all catastrophes from which the entire world suffered. For this very reason, the physical relationship between man and woman labeled as "filthy" or "dirty", even if it was officially done and performed within a legitimate marriage contract.

Saint Trotolian says:

"Woman is the Satan's pathway to a man's heart. Woman pushes man to the "Cursed Tree." Woman violates God's laws and distorts His picture (i.e. man's laws and picture)."

Wieth Knudesen, a Danish writer, illustrated the woman's status in the middle ages saying,

"According to the Catholic faith, which considered the woman as a second class citizen, very little care and attention was given to her."

In 1586, there was a conference held in France to decide whether woman was to be considered a human being or not! After lengthy discussions, the people who attended the conference came to a conclusion that: *"Woman is a human being, but she is created to serve man."* Thus, the conference approved the rights for women as human being, a matter that was in doubt and undecided! Moreover, those who attended the conference did not decide on full rights for the woman, but rather she was a follower of the man and a maidservant to him with no personal rights. This decision was in effect until 1938, where, for the first time, a decree was issued to abrogate all the laws that forbid a woman to conduct her own financial affairs directly and open a bank account in her own name. In England, women remained until 1850 with no citizen-status having no personal rights until 1964 when a decree from Oxford University was issued to declare equality between male and female students.

Europeans continued to discern women and deprive them their rights throughout the entire Middle Ages. It is also surprising to know that English laws permitted the man to sell his wife. The rift between the sexes, men and women, continued to increase, so much so, that women became fully under the control of man. Women were stripped completely of all rights and whatever they owned. All that a woman owned belonged to her husband. For instance, until very recently, women, according to the French law, are not considered capable of making their own financial decisions in their private ownership. We can read article 217 of the French laws that states:

"A married woman has no right to grant, transfer, bond, own with or without payment, without her husband's participation in the sale contract, or his written consent to it, regardless whether the marriage contract stipulated that there should be a complete separation between the husband's and wife's possessions and ownership's of various items."

Despite all amendments and modifications occurred onto these French laws, we can still see how these laws are affecting the married French woman. It is a form of civilized slavery.

Furthermore, a married woman loses her surname (family's name) as soon as she enters into a marriage contract. A married woman shall carry the family name of her husband's. This, of course, indicates that a married woman will be only a follower of her husband and she will loose even her personal identity.

Bernard Shaw, the well-known English writer says:

"The moment a woman marries, all her personal possessions become her husband's in accordance to the English laws."

Lastly, there is one more injustice that has been imposed upon the woman in Western society which is that a marriage bond is made to last forever, in accordance with the legal and religious teachings. There is no right for divorce (according to Catholicism, at least). Husband and wife are physically only separated from each other. This separation may have contributed to all sorts of social decay and corruption, such as having affairs, mistresses, boyfriends, girlfriends, as well as possibly prostitution, homosexual and lesbian relations.

Moreover, a surviving widow is not given the chance to remarry and lead a normal married life after the death of her husband.

For all these reasons collectively, the status of women became very negligent in the "modern" Western society. This led, at a later stage, to the movement in favor of women in the society led by the Western thinkers, lobbyists, human rights activists and educators. These *"thinkers"* demanded absolute equal rights, socially and otherwise, for women in the society.

Chapter Three

Woman's Rights in Islam

Let us here address the status of women in Islam after the quick summary of the status of women in the pre-Islamic societies. We need here to compare the rights to which Islam has entitled women and the rights that other societies granted.

Islam deals with women in a very comprehensive way. We notice that Islam did not limit its care of women to a specific stage of life; but rather, paid close attention to women's needs and rights throughout her life, as we shall illustrate through the following discussion. Islam focused on the female, in general, as daughter, wife, mother and otherwise in the Islamic society.

Daughters in Islam

Allah (﷾), stated in the Glorious Quran 17:31 concerning the necessity and importance of the preservation and care of female and male newborns - which the meaning of is translated as:

"And kill not your children for fear of poverty. We provide for them and for you. Surely, such a killing is a great sin."

In fact, Islam declares that the killing of children is a great sin which is punishable by Allah.

Islam requires the parents to give their children beautiful names, take proper care of them, take care of all their needs, provide for them what they need, in accordance to parent's level of income, and ensure a decent, respected and honorable life for them. Islam imposes this as a child's right. Allah (ﷻ), stated in the Glorious Quran 2:233 which the meaning of is translated as:

"Mothers shall nurse their children for two whole years, for those parents who desire to complete the term of suckling, and the father of the child shall bear the cost of the mother's food and clothing on a reasonable basis."

Nursing and child up-bringing is the most important right after the right of (milk) nursing by the mother. The mother is entitled to the upbringing of the child, son or daughter, at the early stage of life, between the ages of one and thirteen or fourteen. This applies particularly in case of divorce due to essential differences between parents. Islam entitles the mother custody during early childhood because she, generally, is more caring and attentive of the child's need. 'Amr bin Shu'aib related of Allah's Prophet (ﷺ) that: "A woman came to the Prophet (ﷺ) complaining about her husband saying, *'My belly (womb) held my baby as a fetus, my breast nursed the baby as an infant and my lap carried the baby for a long time. The baby's father divorced me, and he wants to strip the baby (my child) away from me!"* He (ﷺ) said *"You deserve the child's custody as long as you do not remarry."*[27] Abu-Bakr (ﺀ), the first rightly guided Caliph of Allah's Prophet (ﷺ), passed a verdict in favor of 'Asim's mother, the wife of

---

[27] This Hadith is reported by Ahmad, Abu Dawood and Baihaqee.

Omar bin al-Khattab (⟨﷽⟩), when Omar divorced her. Abu-Bakr (⟨﷽⟩), said: *"Her smell, the way the mother smells her child, and her kindness is better for him than you."*[28]

If it was not for the commands of Allah (⟨﷽⟩), stated in the Glorious Quran, and the teaching of Allah's Prophet (⟨﷽⟩) in the Sunnah, women would not have been given the preference over men. Allah's Prophet (⟨﷽⟩) was reported as saying,

"Be fair and just in terms of the gifts you offer your children. If I was to give preference to any (gender over the other) I would have preferred females over males (in terms of gifts)."[29]

Moreover, Allah's Prophet (⟨﷽⟩) concentrated throughout his teachings on giving more care and attention to females in general over the male. Females must be treated with kindness, respect, honor, dignity, integrity and their needs must be looked after. Allah's Prophet (⟨﷽⟩) says:

"He whosoever has three daughters, or three sisters, or two daughters or two sisters, and is very kind to them, demonstrating nice company to them and fears Allah in their treatment, will enter Paradise (as a result of his good actions to these females)."[30]

---

[28] This Hadith is reported by Imam Malik in his book *Al-Mouwatta.*

[29] This Hadith is reported by Baihaqee.

[30] This Hadith was reported by Abu Dawood and Tirmithee.

Allah's Prophet (ﷺ) is also reported to have said:

"He whosoever has three daughters and exercises patience with them, feeds them, clothes them according to his own income, they will become like a barrier for him, to protect him from the torture of the Hellfire." [31]

Islamic laws and teachings mandate that parents raise their children in the best manners and offer them a sound, beneficial and healthy education. Ibn Omar (ﷺ), reported Allah's Prophet (ﷺ) as saying, *"The most sinful of you are those who neglect those whom he is responsible to take care of."* [32]

Ibn Omar (ﷺ), reported that Allah's Messenger (ﷺ) said:

"Each one of you (Muslims) is a shepherd (i.e. care taker). And each one of you is responsible for his own herd (i.e. whatever one is entrusted with). A leader, is a shepherd, and is responsible for his own herd. A man is a shepherd of his family, and he is responsible for his own herd. A woman is a shepherd in her husband's home, and she is responsible for his herd. A servant is a shepherd in his master's wealth, and he is responsible for his herd. Each one of you (Muslims) is a shepherd and each one of you is responsible for his own herd." [33]

---

[31] This Hadith was reported by Ahmad.

[32] This Hadith was reported by Abu Dawood and Nasaiee.

[33] This Hadith was reported by both Bukhari and Muslim.

Additionally, Islam commanded that justice in its broad concept is applied amongst all children regardless of their sexes. Allah (ﷻ), stated in the Glorious Quran 16:90 which the meaning of is translated as:

"Verily Allah enjoins justice and doing of good, and liberality to kith and kin, and He forbids all shameful deeds, injustice and rebellion. He admonishes you, that you may take heed."

Allah's Prophet (ﷺ) also said:

"Be just and fair to your children; be just and fair to your children; be just and fair to your children, (three times)."[34]

Bukhari also reported that "'Aishah, the mother of the believers (﷞), said to the prophet 'A poor woman came to my door carrying two little girls. I offered the woman (3) three dates. She gave each of her two girls a date, and lifted the third one to her mouth to eat. Both her daughters asked her to feed them. The woman split the last date into two pieces and gave one half to each of her two daughters.' I admired what the woman had done and reported it to Allah's Prophet (ﷺ), who said upon hearing it:

"Verily, Allah made paradise, a permanent abode for that woman for what she did in terms of sacrifice, and He has liberated her from the hellfire."[35]

---

[34] This Hadith was reported by Bukhari and Muslim.

[35] This Hadith was reported by Muslim.

Undoubtedly, this noble direction of Allah's Prophet (ﷺ) ties together human emotions; i.e., the natural love of children, and the reward in the hereafter. The love of the hereafter is but an incentive for parents to be kind, merciful and just to all their children. Parents will pray for the reward from Allah.

Islam calls for material and emotional justice and fair treatment from both parents to their children, regardless of their sexes. A male child is not to be given preference over a female child, and vise versa. Allah's Prophet (ﷺ) once was asked by a man to give him testimony that he gave his son a certain gift. Upon that, Allah's Prophet (ﷺ) asked the father: *'Did you give all your children the same as you gave this son?''* The man answered negatively. Allah's Prophet (ﷺ) said:

''Let someone else be a witness. I will not bear witness to an unfair and unjust thing. (O People!) Fear Your Lord, Allah, and be just amongst all your children.'' [36]

Islam did not limit justice and fair treatment to visible matters only. This treatment was passed on to all details of the life, including, but not limited to emotional acts such as kissing a child or smiling for him. Anas (ﷺ), reported that a man was sitting with Allah's Prophet (ﷺ). A son of that man came to see him. The man kissed his son and let him sit on his lap (thigh). (A little later), a daughter of that man came (to see her father). He made her sit in front of him. Allah's Prophet (ﷺ) said to the

---

[36] This Hadith was reported by both Bukhari and Muslim.

man: *"Why do you not equalize (in treatment) between both of your children?"*[37]

It is worth mentioning here, also, that Islam emphasized the importance of taking care of the orphans. Being an orphan has a great negative impact on the mental, spiritual and emotional status of a child. This state may lead an orphan to deviation or corruption at times, especially if the orphan exists in a society that does not give him due care, fulfill his needs and be kind and merciful to him.

Islam pays special attention, and gives tremendous care, to orphans, males and females. Islam required that the immediate relatives of that orphan take good care of him/her. If there are no relatives, then it becomes the responsibility of the Islamic State to take care of them, manage their affairs and provide them with care. Allah (ﷻ), stated in the Glorious Quran 93:9 which the meaning of is translated as,

"Therefore, treat not the orphan with harshness."

Allah (ﷻ), also stated in the Glorious Quran 4:10 which the meaning of is translated as:

"Verily, those who unjustly eat up the property of orphans, they eat up only a fire into their bellies, and they will be burn in the Blazing fire!" Allah's Prophet (ﷺ) *is also reported to have said: "O Allah! I declare it a great sin to harm, do injustice, hurt or*

---

[37] This Hadith is reported by Al-Bazzar.

waste the rights of the two weak persons, the orphan and the woman.[38]

Allah's Prophet (ﷺ) is also reported to have said:

"Avoid the seven cardinal sins that may cause destruction. The companions asked: 'O Prophet of Allah! What are these sins?' He (ﷺ) said: "To associate others in the worship of Allah, to practice sorcery, to kill a human soul for no due reason, to deal with Riba (usury), to eat up the wealth of an orphan, to back away in the battle field and to accuse the innocent, chaste, believing women with adultery."* [39]

On the other hand, many other statements of Allah's Prophet (ﷺ) have been reported as urging believing Muslims to sponsor orphans, take good care of them, be kind to them and demonstrate love and affection to them. He (ﷺ) said: *"I and the sponsor of an orphan are like these in Jannah.* (He (ﷺ) pointed out to both index and middle fingers)."[40] He (ﷺ) also said: *"Whosoever places his hand over the head of an orphan with mercy and affection, Allah will record the good deed for this person according to the number of hairs that the person's hand wipes of the orphan's head."*[41]

---

[38] This Hadith was reported by Nasaiee.

[39] This Hadith was reported by Bukhari and Muslim.

[40] This Hadith was reported by Bukhari.

[41] This Hadith was reported by Ahmad. The wording of the Hadith, however, is somewhat different as quoted herein.

Islam also paid special attention to foundlings or illegitimate children who are left without any indication to acknowledge their parents, whether it is a male or a female. The Islamic government is required to take care of such children exactly as an orphan. Two good members, a well taken care of orphan and foundling will be brought up in a decent manner so as they may become normal and beneficial members of the society. Thus, these two members of the society may assume their normal life responsibilities rather than being a burden or curse on the society should they be left without care and affection.

Islam values the opinion of the daughter when it comes to marriage. Moreover, Islam considered the opinion of the daughter in the marriage as an essential condition for the validity of the marriage itself. The daughter, the sister, the granddaughter, or the female in general, is free to accept the person who seeks marriage from her, or reject his proposal. The father, or any other guardian, has no right to force her to accept a person whom she does not want. Allah's Prophet (ﷺ) said:

"A virgin girl must not enter wedlock until she gives permission to do so. And a divorcee, or widow, should be also asked to give approval of the proposing man."[42]

Imam Ahmad also reported 'Aishah (ﷺ), as saying 'A woman came to Allah's Prophet (ﷺ) and said, *'O Prophet of Allah! My father offered me as wife to his nephew (who was an honorable man with a good social status in the society, while we were*

---

[42] This Hadith was reported by Bukhari.

normal people with no recognition) so as to elevate his social status. What should I do?' Allah's Prophet (ﷺ) said, *'The matter is in your hands. If you like you may accept and approve the marriage. If you do not, no one has the right to force you to accept it.'* The woman said, *'I approve what my father had done, but I want to teach other women that their fathers have no right to force them to marry whomever they the fathers want.'*

Islam Cares for the Woman as a Wife

Allah (ﷻ), stated in the Glorious Quran 30:21 which the meaning of is translated as:

"Among His signs is this, that He created for you wives from among yourselves, that you may find repose in them, and He has put between you affection and mercy."

We notice that it is one of the great signs of the Might of Allah (ﷻ), is to create for mankind wives from among themselves so that they are comforted, settled, and can derive satisfaction from one another. They both, male and female, derive comfort, satisfaction, help and assistance from each other and support one another.

A wife, according to Islam, is one of the most essential pillars and the foundation of the entire society. She is the basic foundation upon which a Muslim home is established. Islam grants her certain rights and requires her to perform certain duties as we shall illustrate in the following section.

Dowry

Dowry, is a right of every bride prior to marriage. This is a gift that has been specified and mandated by the Islamic teachings. A marriage contract is not complete unless and until a dowry has been approved. Dowry cannot be dropped or forfeited, even if the bride approves, until the marriage contract is completed. The woman entering marriage has the freedom to do whatever she wants with what she owns after the marriage contract is fulfilled. Allah (ﷻ), stated in the Glorious Quran 4:4 which the meaning of is translated as:

"Give the women whom you marry their dower (obligatory bridal money given by the husband at the tie of marriage) with a good heart, but if they, of their own good pleasure, remit any part of it to you, take it, and enjoy it without fear of any harm (as Allah had made it lawful)."

Dowry is one of the woman's rights. A husband may not, and is not allowed to take anything back of the dower that he has given to his wife if he decides to divorce her and seek another marriage. Allah (ﷻ), stated in the Glorious Quran 4:20-21 which the meaning of is translated as:

"If you intend to replace a wife by another and you have given one of them a 'Qintar' (approx. 100 kg of gold) as dowry, take not the least of it back; would you take it wrongfully without a right and with a manifest sin. And how can you take it back

*while you have gone in unto each other, and they have taken
from you a firm and strong covenant?"*

Allah (ﷻ), also stated in the Glorious Quran 4:19 which the
meaning of is translated as:

*"O you who believe! You are forbidden to inherit women against
their will, and you should not treat them with harshness, that
you may take away part of their dowry you have given them,
unless they commit open illegal sexual intercourse. Live with
them honorably; if you dislike them, it may be that you dislike a
thing and Allah brings through it a great deal of good."*

This verse ensures the wife's rights as illustrated by Allah (ﷻ),
as stated in the Glorious Quran.

It is forbidden and unlawful to inherit women against their will.
We have illustrated earlier that Arabs during the pre-Islamic era
used to inherit the woman herself. If a husband, who had grown
up children who are capable of marrying, died; his widow was
inherited by the elder son from another marriage; or else, that
heir may offer that widow of his deceased father to any other
man. Or, the stepson; i.e., the heir, used to forbid the widow of
his father to marry someone else. This practice that rendered the
widow as a commodity in the hand of the stepson or heir, entitled
the man to do as he wishes with her.

Allah (ﷻ), illustrated in the Glorious Quran that it is unlawful for a man to mistreat his wife in such a fashion that imposes hardship, harassment and burden to her. Such as insulting her, beating her, wasting her wealth and funds or even forbidding her from going out of her house, in an attempt force her to pay all she possesses as ransom to her husband to release her in divorce.

Islamic laws and teachings, however, permit the husband to impose hardship onto any woman who displays distorted moral conduct that is shameful and harmful to the entire society and may cause decay to the social order. A woman who fornicates, for instance, or commits adultery, may be treated harshly so that the man may demand return of the dowry that he gave her when he married her. Afterwards, such a woman may be offered divorce.

Allah (ﷻ), commanded in the Glorious Quran that a husband must live with his wife honorably, kindly and with respect. A man must say and do nice things to his wife. A man must wear decent, clean and acceptable clothes when he sits in his household. A man must look in his best as he likes his wife to do for him at home, because this is only human nature. Allah's Prophet (ﷺ) is reported to have said:

"The most complete believers in terms of faith are those who possess the best morals. The best of you are those best to their wives." [43]

---

[43] This Hadith is reported by Tirmithee.

Allah's Prophet (ﷺ) is reported to have been always pleasant, kind and caring to all. He played and joked nicely and politely with his family members. He was also known to be very kind and good to them. Imam Ahmad reported Allah's Prophet (ﷺ) as saying,

"All things man may play with and have fun are rendered vain and waste of time except three items as follows: to practice archery, to train one's horse and to play and have decent fun with one's wife. These three items are lawful and truthful ones."

Allah's Prophet (ﷺ) spent generously on his family members as he could financially afford. Allah's Prophet (ﷺ) also is well known for being cheerful and decent in joking with his household and playing with them. 'Aishah (ﷺ), the mother of the believers, is reported to have said, "Allah's Prophet (ﷺ) raced with me and I beat him before I become old and heavy. Later, when I became old and heavy he raced with me again and he won. Allah's Prophet (ﷺ) said to me upon winning the race, *"This win of mine makes up for that win of yours."* [44]

Allah's Prophet (ﷺ) is reported to have sat in the house for a short while with his family, talking to them, giving them company and showing kindness, before going to sleep, and after offering the late evening prayer, i.e. Isha. Ibn Abbas (ﷺ) narrated, "I slept at the house of Maymunah(the Prophet's wife) one night

---

[44] This Hadith was reported by Imam Ahmad (RAA).

when it was her night to see the Prophet's night prayer. He (ﷺ) talked with his wife for a period of time then he slept"[45].

Allah (ﷻ), stated in the Glorious Quran 33:21 which the meaning of is translated as:

"Indeed in the person of the Messenger of Allah there is a good example to follow for those who believe in Allah and the hereafter, and remembers Allah much." Hence, Allah's Prophet (ﷺ) is the best example to follow for all of us, the believing Muslims. Muslims ought to follow the pattern of Allah's Prophet (ﷺ) in all of their personal and public affairs throughout their entire life."

Justice, Fairness and Equality

This practice applies to husbands who are married to more than one wife. A husband who has a polygamy marriage in accordance to Islam must be fair and just to all of his wives and treat them on equal terms with regards to feeding, clothing and time-sharing. Allah's Prophet (ﷺ) is reported to have said:

"He who has two wives and does not demonstrate justice, fairness and equality amongst them will come on the Day of Resurrection with one of his sides paralyzed."[46]

---

[45] Reported by Muslim

[46] This Hadith was reported by Tirmithee.

Expenditure

A husband must spend enough of his income and wealth for his wife. He is required to secure suitable housing, daily needs in terms of food, clothing and whatever other necessities the house may require. Allah (ﷻ), stated in the Glorious Quran 65:7 which the meaning of is translated as:

"Let the rich man spend according to his means, and let the man whose resources are restricted, spend according to what Allah has given him. Allah puts no burden on any person beyond what He has given him. Allah will grant after hardship, ease."

Hakeem bin Mu'awiyeh al-Qushairee reported his father as saying:

"I asked Allah's Prophet (ﷺ) 'what is the right of one's wife onto him?' He answered, "Her right is to feed her as you feed yourself, to clothe her as you clothe yourself; do not hit her at the face, do not use insulting language, and do not abandon her bed for any place other than home."[47]

Therefore, if a rich man declines to spend on his family in accordance with his means, and the wife was able to take a portion of his wealth, even without informing him and making it clear to him, she may take a sum that only would satisfy the essential needs of her and her children, without exaggeration or overspending. This ruling is based upon the incident of Hind bint 'Utbah who came to Allah's Prophet (ﷺ) complaining about her husband, Abu-Sofyan, saying, 'My husband is a miser and he

---

[47] This Hadith was reported by Ibn-Hibban and Abu-Dawood.

does not spend enough on me and his children.' Allah's Prophet (📛) said:

"Take whatever suffices you and your children modestly."[48]

If a husband came under heavy financial strain and was incapable of fulfilling his family financial needs, or if he left his wife for an extensive period of time whereby the wife was hurt due to that absence, the wife is entitled to seek court intervention to break that marriage. This is based on a Hadith reported by Abu-Hurairah (📛), as 'Allah's Prophet (📛) was once asked about a husband who does not have sufficient funds to satisfy the living needs of his wife, what should be done about such a marriage?' Allah's Apostle said,

"This marriage should be broken by the separation of the husband and his wife."

Islam urges men to treat their wives kindly and with a caring and sharing attitude. The Apostle of Allah was reported as saying,

"The most complete believers in terms of faith are those who possess the best morals. The best of you are those best to their wives." [49]

Islam did not neglect the mental and emotional rights of women as well. There are many rights in addition to the materialistic

---

[48] This Hadith was reported by Bukhari and Muslim.

[49] This Hadith is reported by Tirmithee.

rights for women. The following are some of these mental and emotional rights for women:

- Women must be protected by man from all immoral people. They should not be exposed to places of moral corruption, nightclubs and other similar places.

- Allah (ﷻ), stated in the Glorious Quran 66:6 which the meaning of is translated as:

  "O you who believe! Ward off from yourselves and your families a Fire (Hell) whose fuel is men and stones, over which are appointed angels, stern and severe, who disobey not the commands they receive from Allah, and do what they are commanded."

- Women should be taught beneficial things for both this world and the hereafter. All their secrets must be kept and preserved. None of their shortcomings should be disclosed to anyone. No private affairs of the woman should be made public or shared as a conversation item even among the most intimate friends. None of the practices a husband does privately with his spouse should be disclosed openly or secretly to anyone, regardless of how close he might be. Allah's Apostle was reported as saying:

  "One of the worst people in the sight of Allah on the Day of Resurrection is a husband who may do private things with his wife, or a wife who does the same with her husband, then one of them discloses that privacy to others." [50]

---

[50] This Hadith was reported by Muslim.

Spending Night and Sexual Fulfillment

This right is one of the most emphasized rights in Islam. The husband is required and obliged by Islamic law to fulfill the sexual rights of his spouse, to ensure the satisfaction of the spouse so as to refrain one's spouse from getting involved in shameful acts, may Allah forbid. A spouse, as any other female, is in a great need for a big heart to love her, care for her, fulfill her natural and physical needs and take care of her instinctive demands.

Islam, in fact, forbids husbands from indulging themselves in matters of physical devotions, like prayers and fasting, in a way that may detract them from attending to their partners' needs, demands and instinctive requirements. Salman Al-Farisi (صلى الله عليه وسلم), reported, "I went to visit my brother in faith, Abu-Darda (رضي الله عنه), upon arrival, I was greeted by his spouse who was wearing very casual house clothes. Seeing that, I asked her, *'What is the matter with you; why are you wearing such simple and casual clothes and not wearing other suitable clothes to please your husband?'* She said, *'Your brother, Abu-Darda (رضي الله عنه), has no interest, none whatsoever, with this world and its affairs. He spends his nights praying and spends the day fasting!'* Upon the arrival of Abu-Darda (رضي الله عنه), who welcomed Salman (رضي الله عنه), and offered him some food, Salman said, *'Why do not you eat with me?'* Abu-Darda (رضي الله عنه), said *'I am fasting.'* Salman (رضي الله عنه), said *'I take an oath by Allah that you must break your fast and eat with me"*. Abu-Darda (رضي الله عنه), broke his fast and ate with Salman (رضي الله عنه). Salman spent that night with Abu-Darda (رضي الله عنه). The latter got up during the night to offer some night prayers. Salman (رضي الله عنه), stopped him from doing so saying *'Your body has certain rights upon you; your Lord has certain rights upon you; and your family has certain rights upon you. Fast some days, and break the fast on others, approach your spouse and fulfill her instinctive needs. Grant every person his due right.'* Just before the break of dawn, Salman (☺), permitted Abu-Darda (☺), to get up and offer prayers. Both of them got up, performed ablution and offered some prayers then they headed to the Masjid to offer Fajr prayer. Upon finishing the prayer with Allah's Prophet (☺), Abu-Darda (☺), reported to the Prophet (☺) what Salman (☺), had said and done to him. The Prophet of Allah (☺) confirmed, *"Salman said the truth."* [51]

The following are some other rights that the spouse enjoys according to Islam:

- A husband must not travel and be away from home for more than a six-month period at one time. (if his wife agree, and this is an estimated period set by the prophet's khalif Omar ibn Al-Khattab (☺) after he consulted his daughter Hafsa(☺) about the period that the wife can stay away from her husband , but, this period remains less or more depends on the wife's sexual demands). A wife, based on her own instinctive nature, may tolerate the absence of her husband for more than six months, or she may demand him to come back before that time. The husband may not refuse or deny his spouse's request unless he has a very valid and legitimate excuse.

---

[51] This Hadith was reported by Bukhari.

- A husband must not make any financial decisions on behalf of his spouse and must not interfere in her own financial affairs unless she gives him such permission. The husband has no right to take any of his spouse's financial assets without her knowledge and approval.

- The husband must consult his spouse insofar as the major household decisions, children's affairs and other mutual affairs. It is not wise to dictate a man's opinion upon all members of the family and not listen to the spouse's opinion, as long as her opinion is wise and correct. Allah's Prophet (ﷺ) gave us a practical example of such doing. On the Day of the Pact[52] the Prophet (ﷺ) commanded his companions to shave their heads and take off their Hajj/Umra garments clothes, "Ihram", but they were slow and did not hasten to fulfill his command. Ummu Salamah (﵂), his wife, recommended that he do so himself and goes out before his companions. Allah's Prophet (ﷺ) acted upon the recommendation of his wife, doing what she suggested and went out of his tent. When the companions saw Allah's Prophet (ﷺ) and what he had done, they all hastened to emulate his act.

- A husband must avoid tracing and counting every innocent mistake his spouse may commit. Allah's Prophet (ﷺ) is reported to have said, *"A husband may not come late at night from a travel to his home without a proper*

---

[52] Peace Treaty of Hodaibiyeh, a well-known place in the outskirts of Makkah where Allah's Apostle (PBUH), concluded a peace treaty with the pagans of Makkah in the 8th year of Hijrah.

notification."[53] A husband may find his spouse in an unprepared situation that he may dislike, and thus this may cause him to dislike his spouse.

- A husband must be kind, tentative, sharing and caring to his spouse. He must deal with her with honesty, decency, patience and care and must take into consideration her very human nature; women like to be loved tenderly and be well taken care of. A husband must demonstrate his affection, love, appreciation, caring, consideration and genuine keenness to his spouse. This must be expressed with words and actions. Allah (ﷻ), stated in the Glorious Quran 4:19 which the meaning of is translated as:

"O you who believe! You are forbidden to inherit women against their will, and you should not treat them with harshness, that you may take away part of the dower you have given them, except where they have been guilty of illegal sexual intercourse. And live with them honorably. If you dislike them, it may be that you dislike a thing and Allah brings through it a great deal of good."

It is also reported that Allah's Prophet (ﷺ) said:

"A believing Muslim must not declare his dislike of a believing spouse. A husband may dislike some of his spouse's behaviors, but he will definitely like others."[54]

---

[53] This Hadith was reported by Bukhari and Muslim.

[54] This Hadith was reported by Muslim.

Islam Cares for the Woman as a Mother

We note that the Glorious Quran greatly emphasized the right of the woman as a mother. In fact, Allah (﷾), stated in the Glorious Quran 17:23 which the meaning of is translated as:

"Your Lord has decreed that you worship none but Him; and that you be dutiful, kind, and caring to your parents. If one of them or both attains old age in your life, say not to them a word of faintest complaint or disrespect, nor shout at them; but address them in terms of honor."

Allah, in this verse puts His right to be worshipped along with the right of parents, in the same address and at the same level. This displays the great rights and position of parents in Islam.

Allah's Prophet (ﷺ) declared that: *"Paradise is under the mother's feet."*[55] No doubt this is a symbolic representation of the fact that the pleasure, caring, respecting and serving the mother will definitely lead man to attain the pleasure of Allah and Paradise, which He promised as a reward for His rightly guided Muslim believers.

---

[55] This Hadith was reported by Al-Nasaiee and Ibn Majah as follows: "A man came to the Prophet (PBUH), and said: "O Prophet of Allah! I intend to participate in the Islamic fighting for the cause of Allah. I came to consult you about it. The prophet (PBUH) asked the man "Do you have a (living) mother? The man said Yes. He (PBUH) said, "Do not depart her sight. Paradise is by her feet."

Mothers, in the first place, before fathers, deserve kindness, caring, good treatment, kind company and best care and service from their children. Abu-Horairah (🙵), was reported as saying:

"A man came to Allah's Prophet (🙵), and asked him: *'O Prophet of Allah! Who is the most deserving and worthy of my good company and care?'* Allah's Prophet (🙵), responded *'It is your mother.'* The man asked, *'Who comes next after her?'* He (🙵) said, *'Your mother'*. Again, the man asked, *'Who comes next after her?'* He (🙵), said *'Your mother'*, The man sked again, *'Who comes next after her?'* He (🙵), said, *'Your father.'*"[56]

This Hadith indicates that a mother has three times the rights that of a father in accordance with Islam. This entitlement is given to the mother due to the tremendous suffering that she goes through during the various stages of the life of her child, in pregnancy, delivery, nursing as well as the shared responsibility of raising the child. The fetus lives, nourishes and thrives on the account of the mother's digested food while in his mother's womb for nine months. Similarly, the nursing baby does the same for two years of his life, if the mother decides to breast-feed her child. This has been illustrated by Allah (🙵), as stated in the Glorious Quran 31:14 which the meaning of is translated as:

"And We have enjoined on man to be dutiful and good to his parents. His mother bore him in weakness and hardship upon

---

[56] This Hadith was reported by Bukhari and Muslim.

weakness and hardship; his weaning is two years. Offer Me thanks and to your parents; unto Me is the final destination."

Mothers, therefore, are given priority over fathers, and anybody else for that matter, in terms of being kind, caring, dutiful, mindful, good, obedient and helping.

Both parents, in accordance to Islamic teachings and principles, are to be obeyed, respected and not differed with as long as they do not command or order their children to disobey their Creator, Allah (ﷻ). If parents ordered their children to perform any act of disobedience to Allah, in any form, shape or size, then they are to be disobeyed in that particular aspect of practice only. In the meantime, a son/daughter must continue to present their normal duties towards parents; they are expected to serve them, help them in their worldly affairs, come to their rescue when they need them. Allah (ﷻ), stated in the Glorious Quran 31:15 which the meaning of is translated as:

"And if parents strive with you to make you join in worship with Me others that of which you have no knowledge, then obey them not, but behave with them in the world kindly, and follow the path of him who turns to Me in repentance and obedience. Then to Me will be your return, and I shall tell you what you did throughout your life."

Obedience to parents must be given priority over all others including the wife. This means, that by no means the wife is to be humiliated, insulted, tortured or otherwise. Each individual must be given his/her due right of respect and obedience accordingly;

however, parents should be given priority in obedience over all others.

Allah's pleasure with man is but an indication of the pleasure of the parents with their son/daughter, and vise versa. His dismay, wrath and displeasure is due to occur as a result of dismaying, displeasing or humiliating one's parents. Allah's Prophet (ﷺ) said:

"Allah's pleasure with man is but an indication of the pleasure of the parents with their son/daughter, and vise versa. His dismay, wrath and displeasure is due to occur to man as a result of dismaying, displeasing or humiliating one's parents." [57]

Caring for parents, being good and kind to them, pleasing them and taking care of their immediate needs, especially in old age is preferred over participating actively and involving physically in the various acts of Jihad, striving for the cause of Allah. Unless every Muslim, male and female, is compelled to take an active part in Jihad activities, the care for parents is given utmost priority in accordance with Islam. Ibn Masaud (ﷺ), reported: 'I asked Allah's Prophet (ﷺ): "O Allah's Prophet (ﷺ) What is the most liked act in the sight of Allah?" Allah's Prophet (ﷺ) said: *"Offering the prayer in its accurate due time."* I, the reporter of the Hadith, further asked: 'What comes next, O Prophet of Allah?' Allah's Prophet (ﷺ) said: *"Being good, kind, respectful, obedient and caring to your parents."* I, the reporter of the

---

[57] This Hadith was reported by Tirmithee.

Hadith, further asked 'What comes next, O Prophet of Allah?' The Prophet said *"Striving, Jihad, for the cause of Allah."*[58]

Abdullah bin 'Amr bin al-'Aas (ﷺ), also reported: 'A man came to Allah's Prophet (ﷺ) and said to him: "O Prophet of Allah! I shall give you my pledge of allegiance to migrate and strive in the cause of Allah seeking His reward only.' Allah's Prophet (ﷺ) upon hearing that asked the man: *"Are your parents alive?"* The man said: 'Yes, O Prophet of Allah, both of them is living." Allah's Prophet (ﷺ) said,

"If you seek the pleasure and reward from Allah go back to your parents and make sure that you do the best you can to serve them, please them, take care of their needs especially at the old age and be good and kind to them."[59]

Parents must be respected, obeyed and offered financial assistance by their children, even if they have different religion or faith, other than Islam, as long as they do not demand that their son/daughter do any act of disobedience to Allah. Asma, the daughter of Abu-Bakr (ﷺ), said: "My mother, who was still a pagan, came to visit with me. I went to Allah's Prophet (ﷺ), seeking his advice on what I should do regarding her visit, despite the fact that my mother was expressing an interest in Islam, 'Should I be kind and good and take financial care of her?' Allah's Prophet (ﷺ), responded,

---

[58] This Hadith was reported by Bukhari.

[59] This Hadith was reported by Bukhari and Muslim.

'Yes, indeed. You should be kind and good and take care financially of your mother even if the mother was a pagan.'[60]

A son/daughter must help and give every possible assistance to parents in their various daily household chores. One must not be aloof and refuse to physically help his parents in their daily regular house activities. Allah's Prophet (ﷺ), himself, used to mend his own clothes, mend his own shoes and help his family with their daily chores. In fact, 'Aishah (ﵻ) once was asked: 'What did Allah's Apostle used to do while at home?' 'Aishah (ﵻ), said, *"Allah's Prophet (ﷺ), used to serve and assist his household; however, when he would hear the call to prayer, he would immediately leave the house.*[61]

Goodness, kindness, obedience and caring for parents' needs must, in fact, be given higher priority over all other voluntary acts of prayer and worship. This is based on a Hadith where Abu-Horairah (ﵻ), reported the Prophet as saying:

"None, except three infants spoke while still in the cradle". These were:

- Jesus son of Mary (ﷺ).

- The second is an Israelite at the time of Juraij. Juraij was a monk isolated himself in a cell and devoting his time for prayer and worship of Allah. One day, Juraij's mother

[60] This Hadith was reported by both Bukhari and Muslim.

[61] This Hadith was reported by Bukhari.

sought him out asking help while he was indulged with his prayers. He said: *'O Allah! I am confused, to whom should I give priority; my prayers or my mother?* He preferred to continue his prayers, and neglected his mother's request for help. Upon seeing that, Juraij's mother left. On the following morning the mother did the same, and Juraij also continued his prayers and neglected his mother's call for help. On the following day, Juraij's mother came again to him and called him to help her, as she had done in the past two days; Juraij did not respond. Upon seeing that, the mother said, *'O Allah! Have Juraij look at the faces of prostitutes before he dies.'* Israelites at the time used to highly admire the amount and manner of Juraij's worship, prayers and seclusion to which he devoted himself. A very beautiful and attractive prostitute that was popular at that time proposed to Israelites, *'If you wish, I can tempt Juraij and cause him to fall in love and commit illegal sexual activities with me'.* The prostitute set out to execute what she proposed. She tried her best to lure Juraij into illegal sex with her; but to her surprise and dismay, her efforts were a failure. Hence, she approached a shepherd who used to stay close to Juraij's cell and offered herself to the shepherd who showed no objection. The prostitute got pregnant. Upon delivery, the prostitute accused Juraij of being the father of the child. The Israelites went to Juraij in his cell, drove him out, destroyed the cell and started beating him. He asked: *"What is the matter? Why are you doing so?"* They said: *"You have fornicated with this prostitute and she delivered a baby from you, while you pretend to be a pious man."* Juraij said: *"Would you bring the baby here and let me offer my prayers, in an attempt to prove to you that I am not the father of that child.*" The Israelites permitted Juraij to offer his prayers, and brought the baby. When Juraij finished his prayers, he went to the baby and pointed to his belly with his hand asking, "*Who is your real father, baby?*" The baby, who was still in the cradle, said, "*My father is the shepherd.*" Upon hearing the baby's statement and confession, the Israelites started kissing Juraij, seeking his blessings and said, "*Should we reconstruct a cell out of gold for you?*" He said, '*No. But just rebuild it of clay and mud as it was built before.*' And so they did.

- The third was an infant who was nursing at his mother's breast when a knight wearing very fancy clothes, passed by on a beautiful horse. The nursing mother said, '*O Allah! Let my son become in the future like this knight.*' Upon hearing this supplication, the nursing infant left his mother's breast and said, while looking at the knight himself, '*O Allah! Do not make me in the future like this knight*". Then, the infant went back to sucking. (The narrator of the Hadith, Abu-Horairah (ﷺ), said: '*I can remember the Prophet (ﷺ) imitating the infant's nursing his mother's breast by placing his index in his mouth and sucking it.*')

"Then the mother and her nursing infant passed by a maid who was beaten by her master and others accusing her with fornication and theft. The maid continued to say, '*Allah suffices me and He is My Guardian!*' The mother said, '*O Allah! Do not let my child be like this woman in the future.*' Upon hearing his mother's statement, the infant left his mother's breast and said, '*O Allah! Let me be like this woman in the future!*' The mother upon hearing her infant's statement addressed him saying, '*Son! What is the matter with you? A nicely dressed knight passed by on a very nice horse, with a high status and power and I wished that you will be like him in the future; you refused to be like him. When we passed by that maid who was beaten and disciplined for an accusation of fornication and theft, and I prayed Allah for you not to be tortured and accused like her; you rejected my supplication also.*' The infant said, '*Mother, As for the knight, he was a tyrant, and therefore I asked Allah not to make me like him. As for the beaten and accused maid, she has neither fornicated nor stolen. Thus, I asked Allah to make me innocent and pure like her!*'[62]

Islamic teachings warn against disobeying parents, disrespecting them and not fulfilling their financial rights. Abu-Bakrah (ﷺ), reported of Allah's Apostle as saying:

"*The punishment for all worldly sins may be deferred until the Judgment Day by Allah except for the sin of disobedience of children to their parents. This sin's punishment shall be imposed during the lifetime of man and not deferred until later.*"[63]

Allah's Prophet (ﷺ) was also reported as saying,

"*Verily, Allah has forbidden you to disobey your mothers, to prevent people from their entitlements, and to ask people for what you are not entitled; He has further forbidden burying your baby-girls while they are alive. He, also dislikes for you to say "Other people said so and so". He, also, has forbidden you*

---

[62] This Hadith was reported by Bukhari and Muslim.

[63] This Hadith was reported by al-Hakim.

to continuously ask others to give you; or to question everything you see; or to waste your wealth for no meaningful reason.[64]

Allah's Prophet (ﷺ) illustrated that being good and kind to parents is essential in the fulfillment of the supplications and prayers of man throughout his life. Ibn 'Omar﷽, reported the Prophet as saying:

"Three men in the previous times set out on a business trip. When night approached they slept in a cave at the bottom of a mountain. Upon entering the cave, a boulder rolled down and closed the cave's entrance completely. They talked it over and concluded that there was no way out of this trouble except with prayers and supplications. *'We had better seek the help of Allah according to the best and most righteous deeds we have done in our lives.'*"

The first man said, *'O Allah! I had two elderly parents whom I never offered my wife and children anything to eat or drink before I offer them. One day I had to go for a long distance seeking food for my herd and I was late coming back. Upon arrival I found both of my parents asleep. I milked the sheep in order to offer my parents their dinner but I hated to wake them up to drink. However, I did not offer my wife or children before I offered them. I remained standing next to them carrying the milk pot in my hand waiting for them to wake up. At the break of day, they woke up, by that time my children were at my feet*

---

[64] This Hadith was reported by Bukhari and Muslim.

crying for milk. At that time, they woke up and I offered them their milk. O Allah! If you know that I have done that for Your sake, please salvage us from this trouble that we are suffering.' Upon that the rock was moved slightly away from the cave's entrance, but it was not enough to let a man out.

The second man said, *"O Allah! I had a female cousin from my father's side who was the most beloved woman to me on the face of Earth. I wanted her very badly to make love to me, but she refused. At one point in time, she underwent a very bad financial problem and came under a lot of financial stress due to famine. She came to me asking for help. I offered her a hundred and twenty 120 golden Dinars in order to let me have what I wanted from her; i.e., illegitimate sexual relations with her outside the wedlock. Under the pressure of her pressing need and poor financial situation, she agreed. When I was ready to begin the intercourse with her, she said, 'O Cousin! Fear Allah! And do not remove the seal of virginity except with the right manner.' Upon hearing that, I got up and did not touch her although she was the most beloved and wanted woman to me. I did not take back the gold which I gave her."* Then he raised his hands to heavens and said, *'O Allah! If You know I have done what I did for Your cause and pleasure, please remove the trouble and the stress that we are suffering. Remove the rock from the cave's entrance so we can get out!'* Upon saying that, the rock was removed a very small distance again, so small as to not enable a person to get out of the cave.

The third man said: *"O Allah! You know that I once employed some workers and at the end of the day I paid their wages except*

*for one who left without collecting his pay. Thus, I rightly
invested his wages in my business and kept a special note and
account for it. The money that belonged to this worker grew a
lot during the years. At one point in time, after many years, the
worker came to me asking for his wage that he did not take for
that day of work. I pointed out to him a large group consisting
of a herd of sheep, cows, camels, slaves and servants, and said
to him: "All that you see is yours! That is the wage that I owe
you!" The poor worker was stunned and said, "Please, do not
ridicule and make fun of me! I am only asking for one-day
wage. The employer said, "I am neither ridiculing you nor
making fun of you. This is all yours." The worker took all that I
pointed out for him and left. Then the man raised his hands to
heavens and said, 'O Allah! If I have done what I did for Your
cause and pleasure, remove the trouble and the stress that we
are suffering.'* Upon that the rock rolled away from the cave's
entrance and the three men left the cave free again." [65]

Islamic teachings also consider the pleasure of the parents, being
good, kind, helpful, considerate, respecting and caring to them as
one of the things that abolishes the sins in this world. It is
reported that Abdullah Ibn 'Omar (؏), said: "A man came to
Allah's Prophet (؈) and said: *'O Prophet! I have committed a
major sin. Do you think that I can repent to Allah from it?'*
Allah's Prophet (؈) asked the man: *"Do you have a mother
living?"* The man answered negatively. Allah Prophet (؈) further
asked the man: *"Do you have a maternal aunt living?"* The man
answered positively. Allah's Prophet (؈) said to him *"Be kind,*

---

[65] This Hadith was reported by both Bukhari and Muslim.

caring, helpful, good, respective and keen to her."[66] This is, of course, due to the fact that the mother's sister (aunt), in accordance to Islam, has a similar position and status to that of the mother. Allah's Prophet (ﷺ) is reported to have said, *"The sister of the mother has a similar position and status to that of the mother."*[67]

Islam required that the rights of parents should continue to be honored and respected even after their death. Malik Ibn Rabee'ah reported, "While we were sitting with Allah's Prophet (ﷺ) , a man from Bani Salamah came to him and asked, *'O Allah's Apostle! My parents passed away. Is there anything required of me as a right of theirs after their death which I should keep and maintain.'* Allah's Prophet (ﷺ) said, *'Yes indeed. You should maintain supplications and prayers on their behalf. Ask Allah continuously to pardon them and forgive them. Fulfill any promises or pledges of allegiance that they have taken or offered others to do. Honor, respect and be hospitable to their friends and maintain a strong ties with your relatives which illustrate your love and respect to your parents."*[68]

All that we have stated and illustrated are only broad guidelines on the major and essential rights of parents, in general, and mothers, in particular, in accordance to Islamic teachings. There

---

[66] This Hadith was reported by Tirmithee.

[67] This Hadith was reported by both Bukhari and Muslim.

[68] This Hadith was reported by both Abu Dawood and Ibn Majah.

are many other rights of parents that we did not state here so as not to bore the reader.

Islam Cares for the Women in General

Islam requires the same rights for women as is required for men. A woman must be extended every possible good thing and have nice treatment. Allah's Prophet (ﷺ) is reported to have said, *"Believers in their mutual care, love and kindness are like one human body; if one organ of that body aches, the entire body will become feverish and man will stay awake all night."*[69]

If a woman is a neighbor and she is a Muslim, she is entitled to two rights: the right of Islam, and the right of a neighbor. Allah (ﷻ), stated in the Glorious Quran 4:36 which the meaning of is translated as:

"Worship Allah and join none with Him in worship, and do good to parents, kinfolk, orphans, the poor who beg, the neighbor who is related to you, the neighbor who is a stranger, the companion by your side, the wayfarer you meet, and those slaves whom your right hand possesses. Verily, Allah does not like those such as who are proud and boastful."

One of the woman's right upon her neighbors is to be good, caring and kind to her. She is also entitled to be protected against various evils of life, supported as needed, respected and cared for. Allah Prophet (ﷺ) said:

---

[69] This Hadith was reported by both Bukhari and Muslim.

"Archangel Gabriel continued to recommend me to take care of the neighbor so much so that I thought the neighbor is going to be my legal heir." [70]

It is also reported that Talhah (رضي الله عنه), said, *"Omar Ibn al-Khattab (رضي الله عنه), went out of his home one night. I decided to follow him to see what he was doing during the night. I saw him entering a specific house. After a while I saw him coming out and entering another house. In the morning I passed by the first house and entered it to check who lives there. To my surprise I found an old, blind and disabled woman. I asked her, 'What did the man who came in your home last night want from you?'* She said, *'This man has been taking care of me for a time, getting me what I need, helping me and supporting me.'* Talha, the reporter said to himself, *"Why should I investigate Omar's actions?"* [71]

Moreover, if the woman was an aunt, from either side, or a relative, regardless of the distance, she is included in the kinfolk to whom Allah commanded to be good, kind and supportive. Allah (سبحانه وتعالى), stated in the Glorious Quran 47:22 which the meaning of is translated as:

"Would you then, if you were given the authority, do mischief in the land, and sever your ties of kinship?"

---

[70] This Hadith was reported by Al-Tirmithee and Abu Dawood.

[71] This Hadith was reported by both Bukhari and Muslim.

Allah's Prophet (ﷺ) is also reported to have said, *"A person who deserts his kinship will never enter paradise."* [72]

Thus we have seen some of the aspects of honoring, respecting, caring and supporting women according to Islamic teachings. Woman, we believe, never witnessed, neither in the past nor in the present, any similar respect and honor throughout the history of mankind on Earth.

---

[72] This Hadith was reported by both Bukhari and Muslim.

Chapter Four

Misconceptions about Women in Islam

There are some misconceptions that have been spread about women and their rights in Islam. These misconceptions were not meant for individual women themselves, but rather an attack on Islam in particular. People who raise such misconceptions aim mainly to distort the beautiful picture of women in Islam. Women, throughout the past fourteen centuries of Islam, have been honored, respected, cherished and dignified. We shall present the main misconceptions that have been raised about women's rights in Islam and women in Islam in general.

Polygamy in Islam

Marriage to more than one wife is a continuation of the practice established and practiced in previous religions. It is a practice as old as history itself. All previous religions practiced, accepted and condoned polygamy. The Old Testament, and the Bible are at the top of the list of the Divine Books that stated such a practice and legalized it. Many previous Prophets, before Prophet Mohammad (ﷺ) entered into plural marriages. Prophet Abraham (ﷺ) had two wives. Prophet Jacob (ﷺ) also had four wives. Prophet Solomon (ﷺ) had many wives. Therefore, we notice that plural marriage, as an issue, is not a new practice attributed to Islam alone. It is indeed an old practice, as old as the history of man on Earth.

It has been stated in the Old Testament,

"A sister should not be taken as a second wife so as one will not harm the other during her lifetime."[73]

Thus, we notice that the Old Testament did not forbid the idea of plural marriage itself, but it rather forbade the man to take a sister of the existing wife as a second wife, while the first wife is still alive[74]. Moreover, the Old Testament stated that Prophet David (ﷺ), had ninety-nine wives. It also stated that Prophet Solomon (ﷺ) had seven hundred wives who were free noble women and three hundred other wives who were slave women.

When Prophet Moses (ﷺ) was commissioned to the office of prophethood he accepted the idea of plural marriage, and did not set or determine a specific number of wives to which a husband was entitled. Later, the people of the Talmud, who lived around Jerusalem, decided upon a certain number of wives for a man. This decision was neither from Moses (ﷺ) nor the Testament. However, some Jewish scholars permitted a second wife or more, if the first wife was permanently ill, or barren. While other Jewish scholars did not permit plural marriages at all.

As for the Bible, we all know that Jesus (ﷺ) was commissioned to complete the Laws of Moses (ﷺ) and we cannot find a single quote in the Bible that forbid plural marriage. In fact, the

---

[73] "The Old Testament and the New Testament", published by American Old Testament Society, and the British Old Testament Society, Cairo, 1938.
[74] Which is also forbidden in Islam

prohibition of plural marriages in Christianity came about as a result of legislation set forth by the Christian church, but not by the original teachings of Christianity itself.

Irish king, Ditharmet, for instance, had two wives.[75]

King Frederick the Second had two wives based on the church's approval. Thus, we notice that "legalization" and "illegalization" was in the hand of the priests of the church and not in accordance with original teaching of Christianity itself.

Martin Luther, the German who established the Protestant sect considered plural marriage an acceptable and condonable principle of Christianity, and in fact he himself advocated it on many occasions.[76]

"Truly, Allah (ﷻ), permitted plural marriage to certain individuals of the Old Testament and in special circumstances. However, the Christian who would like to emulate these individuals is permitted to do so when he is sure that his particular circumstances are similar to the circumstances of those individuals who were permitted to have plural marriages. Polygamy is much better than divorce in any case."

---

[75] Western Mark, (History of Marriage), rendered into Arabic by Abdul Hameed Al-Yunis.

[76] Abbas M. Al-'Akkad, *Woman in the Glorious Quran.*

On the other hand, the modern church under the leadership of the Roman Catholic Pope forbids polygamy or plural marriages. For example:

- The Orthodox forbid either spouse to enter into another marriage as long as the first marriage is still in existence.

- The Orthodox do not permit a second marriage contract for either spouse unless and until the first marriage contract is voided.

- The Orthodox consider the existing marriage an essential reason to forbid a new (second or other) marriage.

Pagan Arabs

Polygamy was well known amongst Arab tribes prior to the advent of Islam. In fact, there was no set limitations for the number of wives the husband can take in wedlock. With the advent of Islam, polygamy was condoned; however, a man was restricted and limited to four wives only. Moreover, Islam set certain rules and regulations to organize, control and regulate this important feature in the social life of Muslims. 'Omair al-Asdee was reported as saying, *'When I accepted Islam, I was married to eight wives. I discussed this with Allah's Prophet (ﷺ) who said, "Keep four only, and divorce the other four."*[77]

Polygamy was also well known to the Egyptians, Persians, Assyrians, Japanese and Hindus. Russians and Germanic people

---

[77] This Hadith was reported by Abu-Dawood.

also practiced it as well as some Greek kings. Therefore, we can see that polygamy is not an invented practice that is known, practiced and applied only by Muslims and authorized only by the religion of Islam. Many other previous nations knew this social practice and applied it.

Polygamy, in accordance with Islamic teachings and practices has its own specific rules, regulations and conditions.

The Main Conditions for Polygamy in Islam

Justice and Equality

As Allah (ﷻ) permitted polygamy, He stipulated and pre-conditioned justice and fairness in treatment, avoiding injustice and wrong practices against all wives. Allah's Prophet (ﷺ) said,

"He who has two wives and does not demonstrate justice, fairness and equality amongst them will come on the Day of Resurrection with one of his sides paralyzed."[78]

Justice and fairness, in this context, applies in terms of material things such as expenditure, fair division of wealth, gifts, time, etc. As for emotional matters, such as love and inclination towards one wife over the other, it is recognized that man has no authority or control over his heart and emotions. Feelings and emotions are involuntary; therefore one is not to be blamed for them. 'Aishah (ﺭ), the mother of believers and the wife of Allah's Prophet (ﷺ) was reported as saying *"Allah's Prophet*

---

[78] This Hadith was reported by Tirmithee.

(ﷺ) *distributed everything justly amongst his wives; yet after all, he used to say, "O Allah! This is the fair way of dividing what I possess amongst my wives. O Allah! Blame me not for what You alone possess while I do not."*, i.e., the heart, feelings and emotions of a man.[79]

Ability to Afford Another Household

If a man knows for sure that he is financially incapable of affording another wife and another household, he is not entitled to seek another marriage. A husband is not allowed to exceed four wives, as stated earlier in the Hadith of Allah's Prophet (ﷺ).

We would like to point out here some of the factors and elements that often urges man to think or seek another marriage. We need to examine whether polygamy in itself is a good or an evil practice in the society. We also would like to know whether such a practice is good for the wife or bad, and whether it is in her interest or against.

1. If a woman is sterile, and the husband is interested in having children, what is best for the wife in such a case: to be divorced for no sin or crime (and become a burden on herself and the society if she cannot earn and there is nobody to support her financially), or to remain in the household of her husband in addition to his other wife?

---

[79] This Hadith was reported by Abu Dawood, al-Nasaiee, Al-Tirmithee and Ibn Majah.

2. If a wife is chronically ill and she cannot perform her marital duties, what is better in her case: to be divorced, or to become a second wife where she is perfectly honored, cared for and provided for by her husband?

3. Some men are sexually demanding. One wife may not be able to fulfill the lawful sexual desire of her husband. Or, if the menstrual period or after-birth-confinement period is especially longer than normal, or she has no lawful sexual desire to match that of the husband, what is better for both husband and wife, in such a case? Is it lawful for the man to seek unlawful sexual satisfaction somewhere else outside the marriage, or to acquire another lawful wife who keeps him chaste?

4. There is no doubt that repeated international and civil wars in various parts of the world has taken its toll on men. Thus, the number of females in most countries is more than males. The best example of that were the First World War and the Second World War, which claimed huge numbers of men who participated in the fighting. Statistics say that there were more than twenty million men killed during these wars. Therefore, if every man had only one wife, what is the destiny of the women who do not get a fair share of lawful marriage to satisfy their needs? Should such women seek to satisfy their sexual desires in unlawful ways like adultery, fornication, and lesbian activities or else? Truly, also, the abundance of women without husbands, or males to care for them, helped spread corruption and illegitimate sexual activities in the society.

5. As a consequence of war also, there are many widows, divorcees and old maids in societies. What is better for such

women in this case: to remain single and suffer all the consequences of life and its demanding needs, or to accept to be a second wife with an honest, protective, honorable and chaste man?

Polygamy does exist in all modern societies. This is a general blanket statement, no doubt, but it is very true and valid one. In all other societies, other than the Muslims' society, polygamy exists in the form of mistresses, sweethearts, girl friends, escort services, common law marriage, etc. These types of polygamy are widespread and have no end of forms. The only difference in that is the title, i.e. the title of the woman. In accordance to Islam, a second wife enjoys all the rights and privileges of the first wife. This is not the case in the modern society man-woman relationships, if it is not a marriage. These types of relationships do not oblige the man (who behaves completely as a husband in terms of co-habitation, marital relations, company, companionship, etc.) to do anything special for such a woman, support her financially, continue his relation with her, etc. Such a relationship has no legal backing (although some countries condone it and accept it as a common practice). This type of relationship between a man and a woman is merely a cheap pleasurable one. It has no merits of its own to stand on. It is meant for the fulfillment of the sexual interest of both parties only. It imposes no financial, social, or emotional obligations on either side at all. If the woman becomes pregnant, it is her own problem, and we all know that a child who is born out of the wedlock is labeled as "illegitimate" child, who is nothing but an added burden on the entire society. Man, generally, is not obliged to admit that the child is his, and is not obliged to take financial responsibility of the child. ·

As for the concept and the practice of polygamy in the Islamic society, it is restricted and limited to four wives only at all times. It must be performed legally and lawfully with a marriage contract, witnesses and the man must bear all financial burdens and responsibilities that arise from this marriage. The husband must pay a dowry for the woman to whom he marries, and must bear all expenses of the wife, her children, and the household. All children of this marriage are legitimate children who must be raised and cared for under the responsibility of both parents.

One may ask, "If we permit polygamy for men, why it is not permitted for women as well!" The answer to this question is as follows: Full equality between men and woman in polygamy is impossible due to natural and physical reasons, as we will explain.

Physically:

Man, in virtually most societies of the world, has the authority over the household. Just for the sake of discussion: if a woman has two or more husbands, who will have the authority and leadership of the house? Yet, again, whose desires shall the woman fulfill, the first or the second man? It is definitely impossible for a woman to fulfill all the men's desires, needs and requests. If the woman preferred one over the other, all will be angry and upset.

Naturally:

Woman can only become pregnant once a year, if any. She can get pregnant by one man only. But, man, on the other hand could have more than one child from more than one woman in the same year, if he has more than one wife. Moreover, if woman is allowed to be married to more than one man, who will be the real father of the child in case of pregnancy, and how would that be determined?

Western Thinkers Demand Polygamy

We would like here to present some statements of the Western thinkers who demanded polygamy and considered it the only solution for many problems of their societies.

Gustave Le Bond, the well-known French thinker says in his book *Arab Civilization, 'Polygamy enables the society social crisis, prevents the mistresses' problem and cures the society from illegitimate children.'*

Anni Peasant, in her book *Indian Religions* says,[80] *'I read in the Old Testament that the closest friend to Allah, whose heart acts upon the Will of Allah, was polygamous.'*

Moreover, the New Testament did not forbid polygamy except for priests or ministers of the church, who were demanded to

---

[80] Al-Azhar University Magazine, Vol.8, page 291.

keep and maintain one wife only. Old Indian religious books also permitted polygamy. It is easy, however, to criticize others in their religious practices. And that what made people accuse Islam and attack it for the permission of polygamy.

However, it is strange that Westerners are against restricted and limited polygamy of the Muslims, while they suffer from wide scale prostitution in their own societies. A close examining look at the Western society illustrates that only a few pure, chaste and honest men respect their clean marital relationships and honor their marriage to one single wife and have no other sexual relationships outside marriage.

It is an incorrect and inaccurate statement, therefore, to prescribe to a community in which the men maintain a single marriage, if they are indeed having mistresses, girl friends and other means of sexual relationships outside the marriage to a legal and lawful wife. If we are to be fair and just, we can see that polygamy in Islam protects, honors, maintains and respects women in the society. Polygamy is better than the Western prostitution that permits a man to have a mistress or a girl friend to fulfill his sexual desires with no respect to the feelings, emotions, needs and honor of the women. The man will disown that woman as soon as he gets his satisfaction. The man has no social commitment or obligation towards the mistress or the girl friend who fulfills his sexual needs and give him the company he needs temporarily. Yes, "it is acceptable to declare that both polygamy and fornication or prostitution are bad and unacceptable, but it is unfair for the non-muslims to blame a Muslim for doing the same thing that he does while his society accepts and condones."

Jawid, the well-known English scholar, says, *"The stiff British system which prevents polygamy is an unfair and unacceptable system. It severely hurts approximately two million women who have become old maids. These women have lost their youth and were deprived having children. Thus, these women were forced to throw away the moral values as one throws the pit of the date."*[81]

Mobenar, a member of the French Parliament noted:

"There are two and a half million French girls now who cannot find a husband, if we assume that every French young man will marry only one woman. I frankly declare what I truly believe is true that 'a woman will not enjoy a healthy life unless she becomes a mother.' I believe that any law which passes a judgment that such a big number of the members of the society should live opposing, contradicting and neglecting to fulfill the natural laws of man on the Earth is but a cruel and savage law that contradicts the simplest meaning of justice and fairness."[82]

In 1959, the United Nations published a special publication illustrating, [83] "This publication has proved by numbers and statistics that the entire world is now facing a growing problem of illegitimate children, as opposed to legitimate children. The

---

[81] Ahmad Abdul Aziz Al-Hussein, *Woman and her Position in Islam.*

[82] Ibid.

[83] Waheed-ud-Deen Khan, *Islam Challenges.*

number of illegitimate children has increased 60% in some countries. In Panama, for instance, the percentage of illegitimate births soared to 75% of the total number of births in the country. This means that three out of every four children are illegitimate, born outside the wedlock. The highest percentage of illegitimate births is stated to be in Latin America. In the meantime, the publication proves and indicates that the number of illegitimate births in the Islamic world is almost nil (in comparison with other countries). The editor of the publication goes on to say 'Islamic countries are protected against such social problems and disease due to the fact that the people practice polygamy.'"

Testimony of Women

Allah (ﷻ) stated in the Glorious Quran 1:282 which the meaning of is translated as:

"And get two witnesses out of your own men. And if there are not two men (available), then a man and two women, such as you agree for witnesses, so that if one of them (two women) errs, the other can remind her."

Allah illustrated in this verse testimonies to assure the rights of others will not be valid unless two men, or one man and two women offer them.

Divine wisdom has granted women, in general, very sensitive emotions, tender feelings, tender care and love. This makes a woman capable of her natural task of childbearing, nursing, taking care of all the needs of the raised child, full custody of the child at the early age of life, etc. These responsibilities require a very big heart, tremendous care, deep emotional involvement and very strong love.

Based on this emotional fact of the woman, she might very well follow her emotional inclinations and swerve from reality, due to her emotional involvement in a case. A woman's loving and very kind feelings might overcome what she has witnessed, and thus she may distort the story of her witness and testimony. Therefore, a divine precautionary measure was established to eliminate any emotional involvement of a woman in any case of testimony or witness in serious, critical and extremely dangerous cases, such as murders and other serious crimes and offenses. If a woman is present at a crime where a murder is being committed, she might close her eyes to avoid seeing such an awful crime taking place. A woman who witnesses such a serious crime also may attempt to run away and escape the crime as well. A woman who witnesses such serious crimes are most likely to be emotionally affected and touched, which may result in loss of temper and composure. This, of course, shall affect the woman's testimony if she is called as a witness to testify about the crime. We would like to point out here also one of the essential principles of the legal and judicial system in Islam which is: "A capital punishment in Islam may be removed, or considered inapplicable, if a doubt arises in the case (or in the crime which is committed)."

Islam has granted women full financial freedom in terms of independence and financial decision making, and made her exactly equal to men in that regard. However, woman's natural role in life, in raising children and caring for the family requires her to stay in the house for longer and extended periods.

It is not as some individuals claim:

"Calling two women testimonies and witnesses is an insult to the woman's intelligence and a dishonor to her integrity." If that were the case, a single woman's testimony would not be acceptable also in the private affairs of women. Islam accepts a single woman's testimony in confirming the virginity of a woman, a delivery of a child, clarification of female sexual defects and other matters which mandate examination of a woman's private parts due to a dispute. On the other hand, Islam rejects one single man's testimony in the least significant financial matters such as lending or borrowing funds and other transactions. In fact, the previously stated cases of acceptable single women's testimony are far more important than what men are shoulders in that area. Therefore, we should realize that a single woman's testimony in serious matters is established in order to preserve and prove the due rights of various individuals in the society, based on that testimony.

Moreover, we would like to point out here that testimony in itself is not a privilege or an honor. It is rather a burden that many male and female attempt to avoid in any society. Therefore, Allah commanded people to offer their testimonies and not to try to escape or withhold it, as they will be asked about it on the Day of Judgment. Allah (ﷻ), stated in the Glorious Quran 2:281 which the meaning of is translated as:

"And the witnesses should not refuse when they are called on (for evidence)."

The address here is general, for both male and female. Many people all over the world try to avoid becoming a witness and attempt not to be involved in offering testimonies due to the fact that there is a great burden and bother in that. One is required to go to the court, sit on the witness stand, take an oath to tell the truth, be cross-examined and many other burdens. Financial and physical burdens may result from offering witness and testimony. A witness may be assassinated in some odd cases. Islam therefore aims at eliminating many of these burdens from the woman in terms of testimony.

In Islam a woman is not required to spend on the family and take charge and become financially responsible for the household (unless she wants to participate willingly), as this is the responsibility of the man. Islam meant for the woman to dedicate herself, her soul, her time and her efforts to the major task of "the maintenance of the human race and the generations."

One man's testimony, on the other hand, is not acceptable in financial matters. There should be two male witnesses to prove the financial right of a claimant. No one, that we know of, considers this act as an insult on the man's intelligence and contrary his rights.

Moreover, Islam considers the testimony of a wife exactly equal to the testimony of her husband, when a husband accuses his wife with committing adultery if he has no evidence. Allah (ﷻ) stated in the Glorious Quran 24:6-9 which the meaning of is translated as:

"As for those who accuse their wives, but have no witnesses except themselves, let the testimony of one of them be for four testimonies (i.e., testifies four times) by Allah that he is one of those who speak the truth. And the fifth (testimony) (should be) the invoking of the Curse of Allah on him if he be of those who tell a lie (against her). But it shall avert the punishment (of stoning to death) from her, if she bears witness four times by Allah, that he (her husband) is telling a lie. And the fifth (testimony) should be that the Wrath of Allah be upon her if he (her husband) speaks the truth."

Financial and Moral Responsibilities of the Household

Allah (﷾) stated in the Glorious Quran 4:34 which the meaning of is translated as:

"Men are protectors and maintainers of women, because Allah has made the one of them to excel the other, and because they spend (to support them) from their means."

Financial and moral responsibilities of a household require a strong personality, precision and decisiveness in decision-making, etc. Managing, directing and running the household affairs, in accordance with Islam, is the man's responsibility, and not the woman's. The physical and mental make-up of men qualify them to take charge of these responsibilities. This responsibility is granted to man due to natural qualifications, as explained earlier, and due to earned reasons as well. Man, in accordance with Islam, is required to take care of the household financially, physically, emotionally and otherwise. Man, in accordance with

Islam again, is demanded to protect the woman, take care of her needs, and secure all the needs of the entire household. The man is a responsible "guardian" of his own household, and he will be asked about "his herd", so to speak, as we have been taught by Allah's Prophet (ﷺ).

A woman, on the other hand, is weaker in comparison with man. Due to many things that happen to her physically and take place during her lifetime such as bearing children, delivery, nursing, child-care and custody, etc. She is not as qualified as man to take charge of the entire household responsibilities. This is, of course, no insult to her at all.

Menses, additionally, affect women drastically due to the amount of blood loss every month. Pregnancy subjects women to tremendous pain and sufferings (but it still enjoyable and wanted by most women on Earth). During pregnancy, women are more fatigue and the slightest effort will negatively affect them. During pregnancy, women are more concerned with the fetus than their own selves. A pregnant woman also worries about her delivery, whether it is going to be a normal delivery or cesarean section where she suffers a surgery in addition to the suffering of the pregnancy itself. Also, a pregnant woman expresses too much concern with the welfare of the baby whether such a baby would be normal, healthy or else. All these concerns affect the mentality of a woman and will be reflected in her life, attitude and behavior.

Childbirth

Women require a confinement period for rest after delivery. Women suffer a lot of pain throughout their pregnancy and delivery. The after-birth confinement period calls for a full rest mentally and physically for a period that varies from a woman to a woman.

Child Nursing

A nursing mother donates or gives a certain portion of her digested food to her nursing child. This process affects the nursing mother's health. Many nursing women suffer hair loss, anemia, dizziness and general fatigue during the nursing period (that could last until the child is three years old if not weaned). Moreover, childcare and custody require a lot of effort and hard work from the mother and it is a very time-consuming process.

'Abbas Mahmoud al-'Akkad, the well-known Egyptian writer, notes:

"Women have a very special emotional make-up that does not resemble the emotional make-up of man. The companionship of a little infant or child requires a lot of similarity and resemblance between the child's mentality and his companion, the mother. She has to understand what he wants, what he needs and how he thinks and feels. Therefore, and based on these facts, a woman is much more responsive to emotions. This

makes it difficult for a woman when compared with man in terms of being firm, fierce and determined when needed. [84]

Dr. Alex Liberelle, a Nobel Prize winner, says while illustrating the natural organic differences between man and woman: [85]

"Matters that differentiate between man and woman are not limited to sexual organs, the presence of the womb and pregnancy. These matters are also not limited to the difference of teaching methods of man and woman. In fact, these differences are of basic nature. The tissues of the body in both male and female are different. The chemistry of the bodies is also different in both. Certain glands excrete certain secretions that are only suitable for a specific gender. The woman is completely different from man in terms of the chemical material secreted from the ovary inside the woman's body."

Those who call for complete equality between men and women do not understand these basic facts and essential differences (or else they ignore them). Callers and defenders of women's equal rights demand the same type of education to be given to both male and female regardless of their sexes, and to be offered the same type of jobs, tasks, responsibilities and positions. Woman's nature and essential physical make-up, however, differs completely from that of man. Every body cell of the woman has a feminine quality. Due to this reason, we see that the organs of both men and women are different from each other completely.

---

[84] *Woman in the Glorious Quran.*

[85] Waheed-du-Deen Khan, *Islam Challenges*, page 168.

The same applies on the women's nervous system as well. We must realize that the rules and regulations of the nervous system are strict and accurate as that of the astronomical rules and regulations. They are extremely precise. There is no way to alter, modify or change these rules and regulations. We must accept these rules and regulations as they are and not attempt to change them. We should not seek any unnatural imposition on them. Women must build up their talents based on their own natural gifts, and they must not imitate men."

There is another point that we should bring up here. The muscles of men are naturally more powerful than those of women. This is a well-established fact. Men can perform more tedious, tiring, laborious and manual jobs, while women, most of the times, are not prepared for comparable work performance. Thus, men are more naturally equipped and qualified to assume the role of leadership over the household in general, and over women, in particular.

Women's Right of Inheritance

Allah (ﷻ), stated in the Glorious Quran 4:11 which the meaning of is translated as:

"Allah commands you as regards your children's (inheritance); to the male, a portion equal to that of two females..."

Those who misunderstood Islam claim that Islam does injustice to women in terms of inheritance. How could it be fair to grant the male (son) a portion equal to two portions of that of the female, (although they are brother and sister of the same parents)? Allah (ﷻ), offered a full and detailed method of women's inheritance in the Glorious Quran. Allah has stated three cases for women's inheritance as follows:

- *A woman will have an equal share as that of the man.*

- *A woman will have an equal share to that of the man, or maybe a little less.*

- *A woman will have half the share of man, which is the most common case.*

Those who are interested in further details about this subject may review lengthy discussion in the books about inheritance in Islam. In fact there is a special branch of Islamic knowledge called "Estate Division Science" that deals with all the different ways of dividing an inheritance, the proper share of all relatives which called "Estate-Division and Inheritance" close and distant, etc.

In fact, one must be fair and just. Prior to passing any judgment about "unfair treatment of Islam to women in terms of inheritance", one must examine this subject closely, before making any comment. The following is a simple example of the way Islam passes a verdict to distribute the wealth of deceased among his heirs:

"A man passed away leaving a son and a daughter. The deceased left a sum of US$ 3000.00 for his heirs. In this case, and in accordance with Islamic rules of estate division, the son is entitled to $ 2000.00 and the daughter's share is $ 1000.00."

Let us examine the heirs' situation after the death of the father. The son's share of inheritance is decreasing because he has to pay a dowry (if he intends to get married). He is also required to furnish his house for the marriage and he is also required to take care of all the needs of his household in terms of their expenses. The son is also required to take care of his widow mother, grandparents (if still alive) and other poor and needy relatives. The daughter, on the other hand, is not required to spend any of her inherited money (unless she pleases), even if she is a wealthy and rich person. If she gets married she is entitled to a dowry from her husband. The husband is required to secure all her financial needs as well, in terms of house expenses, health care, childcare and all other financial obligations of the family.

Therefore, it is the man's responsibility to take care of all the financial needs of the woman and his entire family according to his means. The daughter portion of inheritance will increase, rather than decrease, if she gets married and receives a dowry from the husband. She will be entitled to all living expenses in terms of accommodation, food, health-care, child-care and all, from her husband. Man, however, is even required to pay alimony and child support, in case of divorce or separation. A female heir is entitled to do as she desires with her wealth, funds and money. She may invest her share of the inheritance or do as she please with it. Thus, this example illustrates that the daughter's share of the inheritance remains intact, while the man's share is spent for many lawful and valid reasons due to financial responsibilities and obligations that he undertakes in this life. The woman, at least theoretically, is entitled to maintain her share of the inheritance.

Islamic laws and teachings differ from all other national and international legal systems all over the world. In some societies, the father does not carry any financial responsibilities for his own daughter, or son for that matter, after a certain age. The son and daughter are required to take care of their own financial needs and arrangements. According to Islam, a father, (or even a brother after the death of the father) is required to take care of the entire financial needs of a daughter (or sister) until she is married. From the time a female marries, her financial responsibilities are her husband's obligation, according to Islamic teachings. In the meantime, laws that equalize the inheritance share for both male and female heirs require them to bear equal financial obligations and responsibilities as well.

Therefore, demanding a "fair", "just" or "equal" share of inheritance to both male and female Muslims who do not have equal financial obligations and responsibilities is an unfair and unjust demand. Thus, it is only fair and just to give preference to a male heir, in light of the previous discussion, over the female heir from the inheritance of the father, mother or else according to Islam. Man and woman, according to Islam, do not shoulder the same financial obligations and responsibilities. Therefore, it will be unfair to grant them equal inheritance, as decided upon by Allah (ﷻ). Allah (ﷻ), relieved woman from all financial stresses, constraints, responsibilities and obligations, and honored the woman by making her entitled to get all what she needs, have her attended to by her husband, brother, or son. All male members of the family are required and obliged to bear any financial burden of the female members of the family. Yet, a female is entitled, by Islamic laws, to a half share of the portion of that of the male inheritance. This is only fair and just, we believe.

One important thing we should point out concerning the law of inheritance of Islam is that "every male and/or female heir has a specified share of inheritance that he/she is entitled for; and one cannot deprive the heir his/her share of the inheritance." This is unlike the British Law which can grant the owner freedom insofar as his bequest is concerned based upon a will he/she makes before his/her death. Such a will may deprive all the legal and lawful heirs from the inheritance of their relatives. However, in accordance with Islamic teachings, man is entitled to limit only one third of his/her legacy in a will, and cannot exceed this set limit.

Moreover, in accordance with Islam, all expenses resulting from "blood-money" are shouldered by the men of the family. Women do not bear the responsibility of the "blood-money".

Gustave Le Bond says in his book *Arab Civilization*:

"The principles of inheritance which have been determined in the Glorious Quran have a great deal of justice and fairness. The person who reads the Glorious Quran can perceive these concepts of justice and fairness in terms of inheritance through the verses I quoted. I should also point out the great level of efficiency in terms of general laws and rules derived from these verses. I have compared British, French and Islamic Laws of

inheritance and found that Islam grants the wives, whom are considered by Westerners to be ill-treated and that Muslims are not fair in treating their wives (and women in general) are entitled to inheritance rights that are lacking in our laws."

Blood Money

Islam stipulates that blood money is to be paid for a woman's murder as half of that which is paid for a man. This is of course when a Muslim woman is killed by accident, rather than a capital crime.

As for murder, which requires capital punishment, both male and female are equal in the sight of the Islamic laws in this case, as both male and female are equal in terms of human rights. However, in the case of accidental killing where the blood-money paid to the heirs of the victim is half of that paid for a man's killing, it is due to the damage done to the family of that man after his death. The family whose breadwinner is killed loses the person who is financially responsible for the entire family, although a man's emotional care of the family is not comparable to that of the woman's.

As for the family members whose mother is killed accidentally, they only miss, mainly, their mother's love, caring and affection, matters which most men cannot provide. However, the financial situation should not be effected that much with the loss of the mother. Of course, there is no wealth or financial compensation which can substitute for a mother's love, caring and affection.

The blood money in itself is not a price, a value or even a true compensation for the killed person. It is only the least assessment of the damage caused to the family of the killed person, whether it is a father or a mother of a family. Thus, the blood money set forth for a woman to be half of that determined for the man is self-explanatory.

Women's Right to Work

Allah (﷾), created all of mankind from a single male and female. He, also placed love and affection for one another between them, so as to cooperate to construct this world the way we see it now. He, (﷾), specified man, the male, with power, strength and endurance in order that he may seek provisions. In the meantime, Allah (﷾) specified the female, the woman, and equipped her with what it takes to reproduce the progeny of mankind. She is well equipped with necessary apparatus to bear children, deliver them, nurse them and care for them.

Consequently, the woman has been endowed with love, kindness, care, sympathy, care and affection in order to carry out her hard duties with a smile on her face and with pride and dignity. Thus, based on this natural preparation and delegation of responsibilities, and based on the unique specifications of both male and female, it is only natural for man to be prepared to work outside the house, and earn the bread of the family. On the other hand, it is only natural for the woman, the female, to work inside the house and take care for its needs in general.

Islam does not, however, deprive the woman from the right to work. In fact, Islam permits the woman to directly conduct her business contracts and financial transactions. All such contracts and transactions are sound and valid in the sight of Islamic Laws and teachings and they are in no need of the approval of the husband, the father or any other guardian. Islam, however, organized these transactions and set rules and conditions for them. If any of these set conditions is not observed, the permission given to the woman to practice this right will be rendered null and void, and the woman will become forbidden to use her right.

- Woman's work outside her house must not conflict with her duties and responsibilities inside her house, for her husband and children. As we all know, woman is entitled to certain specific rights from her husband, and man is entitled to a certain and specific rights from his wife. Both also owe their children certain and specific rights that must not be wasted either.

- A woman must work with other women. She must not work in a co-ed. environment where she comes into physical contact with other men.

Lady Cook, the well-known English writer says in New Echo:

"Men like (and prefer) the co-ed. environment. Thus, women are lured to something that contradicts with their human nature. The greater the co-ed. environment (between male and female),

the more illegitimate children the society will have and produce. There is the greatest disaster...[86]

In his book, *International Peace and Islam*, late Sayed Qutub says:

"It is the right of both man and woman, to feel satisfied with each other as companions. Neither one of them should be subjected to temptation by the other in such a way that one would be emotionally (and physically) deviated, if not dragged fully into sin and drift towards immoral decay. Such actions will definitely threaten the precious and holy ties between them. In fact, there will be no room for trust and confidence in one another. The deviation resulting from this morality drift is due to the co-ed. relationships which appear to be increasing day by day. As women walk freely wearing all kinds of attractive, short, tempting clothing, that do not modestly cover their bodies but rather show their attractions, wicked minded men, people with low moral values and people with weak faith will abuse women and attack their chastity. Regardless of what some individuals say about co-ed. environments, as it softens the hearts and minds of people. It is a real threat and danger to morality and moral values of the society. Regardless of what they claim, as co-ed. provides both sexes with the necessary experience that is needed for a long lasting marital tie, it is really nothing but nonsense. Many marriages are failing and ending with divorce and broken homes even after full knowledge of one party to the other. Many are the illegitimate sexual relationships in societies

---

[86] Abdur Rahman Wasil, *Youth Sexual and Emotional Problems under the Lights of the Islamic Jurisprudence*, Dar-ul-Shorooq, 1406 H.

that believe in co-ed. as a way of life. The percentage of pregnant high school girls, as a result of a free co-ed. society reached 48% in one high school in the United States. A look at the broken homes which were erected on the so called love and free choice, increased drastically between the years of 1890 and 1948 as follows: 1890 = 6%, 1900 = 10%, 1914 = 14%, 1930 = 14%, 1940 = 20%, 1946 = 30% and in 1948 = 40%, and it is still on the rise."

- The job or the work that the woman performs outside her house must be, in the first place, a lawful job that suits the nature of the woman. A woman, for instance, must not be involved in heavy industrial jobs, actual combat in a military, and other jobs to which men are more inclined such as sewer cleaning, general maintenance, street cleaning, road construction, etc.

The question that poses itself here is: Why does the woman work?

If a woman is working to earn her own living expenses, Islam has preserved this right for her. Islam obliges the father to take care of the entire financial needs and obligations of his daughter until she marries. Upon marriage, the woman's financial needs and obligations (and her children's needs) must be born by her husband. If the husband dies, while the father of the wife is still alive, then the father must resume the financial responsibilities of his daughter, and her children, again, as he did before her marriage. If the father is no longer living and the woman has children who are adults and earning, then the financial needs and responsibilities of the mother becomes her son's. If woman's children are minors and cannot provide for the family, then, the financial obligations and responsibilities of the widow must be born, in accordance with Islam, by her brothers, if they are available. If the woman has no brothers, then her financial responsibilities lie with the nearest of kin and relatives. Therefore, we notice that woman's financial needs, (at least theoretically and in accordance with the Islamic teachings) are assured for her from life to death, throughout her entire life, and she is not demanded to work. This is mainly done and arranged for the woman to concentrate on her most paramount social mission and duty; to take care of the house, to raise children, to take good care of the needs of the entire family members, a mission which requires great efforts, many sacrifices and devotion.

The well-known English scholar Samuel Smiles, one of the pillars of the English renaissance says[87]:

"The system that has required women to work in factories and industrial areas, regardless of the national wealth it brings, has destroyed the family life. It has attacked, in fact, the basic structures and foundations of the house and destroyed the essential pillars of the family. It has cut and destroyed social ties as well. Stripping the wife from her husband (by spending long hours working in factories), and depriving children of their rights for proper tender and maternal care, has resulted in lower moral values for the woman. The real job and profession of a woman is to raise a good, sound and moral family. She is

---

[87] Mostafa Al-Ghalayenee *A Look at Women Purdah*, published in Beirut, 1346 H., pages 94-5.

mainly required to take care of house responsibilities, home economics and other domestic needs. Work in factories has stripped the woman, as we pointed earlier, of all these responsibilities which changed the looks and the realities of inside the home. Children, as well, were often neglected and raised with no sound standards. The love and affection between husband and wife were somewhat extinguished. The woman no longer became the sought, wanted, admired and loved to man, after he got used to seeing her in the factory next to him doing the same thing he does. Woman became under many influences and pressures that changed her mentality and thinking pattern on which moral values and virtues were established."

In fact, the First Lady of South Africa calls for the return of woman to the home saying:

"The most natural place for woman is her own home. The main task and responsibility for a woman must be to care for her husband and attend to the needs of her children." [88]

She also said in an address to a women's conference in the capital of South Africa:

"The main task and responsibility for a woman must be to care for her husband and attend to the needs of her children... This is our duty in society. It is a duty in which we should take special pride as it produces successful men and sound generations."

---

[88] Abdullah bin Wokaiyel Al-Shaikh, *Woman's Work on the Scale.*

Divorce Power Is with Man

We have to realize, in the first place, that Islam hates and dislikes divorce. Allah's Prophet (ﷺ) says:

"The most hated and disliked act in the Sight of Allah, although it is lawful, is divorce."[89]

He (ﷺ) was further reported as saying:

"May Allah (ﷻ), curse a man who often practices divorce after each new marriage."[90]

Islam, on the other hand, mandates that preliminary solutions must be sought for most disputes that occur inside the house between a husband and a wife in order to avoid divorce. Allah (ﷻ), stated in the Glorious Quran 4:128 which the meaning of is translated as:

"And if a women fears cruelty or desertion on her husband's part, there is no sin on both of them if they make terms of peace between themselves; and making peace is better..."

The most natural and logical way to this peace is to let the man have control over the divorce process, and not the woman. Man

---

[89] This Hadith is reported by Abu Dawood and Al-Hakim.

[90] This Hadith is reported Al-Tabaranee. The wording of this Hadith, however, is "Allah dislikes those who marry woman just to taste how they feel like..."

is financially obliged to take care of his wife, household and family. The man is the one who pays the dowry, bears the financial responsibilities and burdens of the entire household, under normal conditions, and takes care of housing and accommodation, ...etc. Thus, he should be theoretically entitled to terminate the marital life if he is willing, ready and prepared to take such a huge loss financially and emotionally that results from a divorce. The husband must be fully aware that he will lose the dowry he spent for the marriage, the alimony and child support, and the expenses of a new marriage.

Additionally, man is more capable, theoretically, of controlling his temper, emotions and personal reactions if upset about large or small issues in life, especially in terms of disputes with his wife. The husband should never seek divorce as a first solution to end his daily suffering with his wife. Divorce to man is the final solution when life becomes catastrophic, meaningless, problematic and can no longer be tolerated with his wife.

However, the woman has the right to divorce herself from her husband in accordance to the Islamic teachings, provided that she has stipulated this before consummating the marriage, and the husband approves it.

Moreover, Islam permits the wife to be divorced from her husband upon request if the husband abuses her by using foul language, insulting manner of speech or beating. Also, she will be entitled to divorce if the husband is impotent and cannot perform his marital duties, or if he chooses not to have sexual intercourse with his wife and fulfill her needs, or if he contracts a terminal illness after the marriage, or he contracts syphilis or any other venereal diseases that may harm the wife or, at least, make her loose her desire to be with that man.

Islam conveys a perfect understanding and appreciation of human nature. Woman, in certain incidents, is given the right to seek separation from her husband, exactly as man has the right. If a wife reaches the extreme limits and hates her husband wholeheartedly and feels she can no longer live with him in any circumstances, then she has the right to divorce. This form of divorce is called "Khul'a"; it is made at the insistence of the wife who must pay compensation to her divorced husband. A Muslim judge will look into the case if the husband refuses to accept the wife's request. In most cases, the judge will pass a sentence in favor of the women.

Women's Inequality to Approach Man Directly for Marriage

Selecting and choosing the right and most suitable wife is a very difficult task. It is, however, much more difficult to choose and select a husband. Furthermore, the husband may be able to seek divorce from his wife if he realizes that she was not suitable. This practice, however, is not as easy to achieve for a woman.

Woman remains the weak side in all human societies. Islam therefore exerts every effort to protect the woman, preserve her rights and seek every possible means to take care of her. Islam demands the father, the mother, the uncles from both sides, the grandfathers, brothers and all other relatives to help select, choose and pick the right and most suitable husband for their females. The woman must not be the victim of a failed marriage because she will suffer the most harms. Islam therefore requires a guardian for the female, a "Wali", in order for the marriage to be sound and valid in accordance with Islamic teachings. If a guardian is not readily available, a substitute must be sought. Allah's Prophet (ﷺ) stated,

"A marriage is not valid without a guardian [for the woman]."[91]

A guardian, usually, is concerned with his ward and her well being. This, by no means, is a denial of the woman's freedom to do what she likes, i.e. to choose and select her own husband. Islam, indeed, has granted the virgin woman, as well as the divorcee and widow, the right to accept or reject any person who proposes to marry her. Islam does not permit the female's guardian, whoever he might be, to impose or apply pressure on her to force her to accept any person who proposes a marriage, or even to reject such a proposition. Physical or mental pressures are not condoned in terms of requesting or forcing the female to get married. This is based on the statement of Allah's Prophet (ﷺ):

"A divorcee (or a widow) must not be wed unless she is asked permission (and approval). And a virgin woman must not be wed (or offered for marriage) unless she is consulted."[92]

---

[91] This Hadith is reported by Ahmad, Abu Dawood and Al-Tirmithee.

[92] This Hadith is reported by Bukhari and Muslim.

If a woman is forced to accept a marriage, she is entitled, in accordance to Islamic teachings, to present her case before a Muslim judge to seek a verdict. This is based on the statement of Allah's Prophet (ﷺ), when a woman, called al-Khansa bint Khitham, came complaining to him that her father made her marry someone (just to remove a shame he suffered due to the fact that she was divorced. The (divorcee) woman came complaining to Allah's Prophet (ﷺ), that her father forced her to marry, although she was divorced, and she hated that marriage. Allah's Prophet (ﷺ) disapproved of that marriage and considered it invalid."[93]

Similarly, Islam requires the acceptance of the woman and her approval of the marriage to a certain man, as it requires the presence of a male guardian for the marriage validity in order to complete a marriage contract.

Islam truly urged Muslims to marry and encouraged Muslims to seek settlement in a marriage. The major goal of marriage in accordance with Islam, however, is to establish an everlasting relationship between a male and a female rather than a temporary relationship that aims at temporal and quick satisfaction of any kind. The female, i.e. the wife in this case, is the second partner in this partnership, hence, her acceptance, approval and condoning of the marriage is also required.

---

[93] This Hadith is reported by Bukhari, Abu-Dawood, Ibn Majah, Al-Nasaiee and Al-Tirmithee.

However, as women are more emotional, in general, than men, and are easily affected with various matters around them, and in common, women are easily tempted with the appearance of things, rather reality of things, Islam gave the right to the guardian to refuse and reject a person who proposes to marry a woman if he is not a sound match for her. Generally, men are more acquainted with other men than women. A man is more capable of finding out more about the characteristics of a man than a woman. But, if an appropriate man who is a sound and good match for a woman proposed marriage but the guardian refused for no valid reason except being stubborn or impossible, then the guardianship will be withheld by Islamic law, and will be given to the nearest male relative of the woman. If the woman has no male relatives, then the Muslim Judge will assume the responsibility of guardianship for that woman and offer her in marriage to the person who proposes marriage to her.

Islam forbids the woman to marry a man who is not a sound and good match for her in terms of social status as such a marriage might bring shame and indignity to the family. Moreover, a forced marriage that is not done with the family's approval will end up splitting the family members and cutting relationships, a matter that Islam does not condone or promote. Allah (﷽), urges Muslims to maintain, support and strengthen family ties as much as possible.

Muslims believe that the true measurement of a matching marriage is the statement of Allah's Prophet (ﷺ):

"If a person accepts his commitment to Islam and is of good morals standards proposes a marriage to you, then grant him the requested marriage. If you fail to do so, great affliction will take place on earth and corruption will be widespread."[94]

A man with a sound and good understanding to his Islamic commitment, and good moral standards will honor his wife and dignify her if he loves her. Such a person will not humiliate his wife if he does not feel a true and deep love for her after marriage.

Travel Without Immediate Male Escort

Islam forbids a woman (single or married) to travel alone without the escort of an immediate unmarriageable relative companion [Mahram] such as a husband, a son, a brother, a father, a nephew, an uncle, etc. Such a relative, other than the husband, must be one of those whom she permanently cannot marry due to his immediate blood relationship to her. Allah's Prophet (ﷺ) said:

"A woman must not travel alone without a male companion of her immediate relatives to whom she can never get married [mahram]. Any man must not enter the house of a woman unless

---

[94] This Hadith is reported by Tirmithee. Failing to honor the request of a person with good faith, practices, morals and character to marry, upon his request, may lead to moral corruption in the society and the community. Such a person may deviate from the clean and normal path of preserved and respected family practices and may go astray seeking to fulfill his sexual desires by unlawful means. This is what the general meaning of the Hadith of Allah's Prophet means.

there is a male relative (Mahram[95]) in the house." A man stood up and asked Allah's Prophet (صلى الله عليه وسلم), 'O Allah's Apostle! My wife set out on a Hajj, pilgrimage trip, while I have registered my name to participate in a battle, what should I do?' Allah's Prophet (صلى الله عليه وسلم), said, "Go and perform Hajj with your wife."[96]

Perhaps a person will argue that this regulation restricts the freedom of the woman and overrides her rights. This is what jumps to mind right away. If, however, we understand the reason behind it we may change our opinion. We can easily remove this misconception about Islam if we realize that Islam intends to maintain and preserve the dignity of the woman and not the opposite. Traveling, generally, requires many hardships. Women, by nature, are, at least physically, weaker than men are, as we illustrated earlier. This is due to reasons of pregnancy, menses, child nursing and childcare. Women are also weaker psychologically than men. They are easily inclined to follow their emotions rather than facts. Women also are easily affected with environment and surroundings.

Therefore, a woman is in need for someone to care for her, protect her and maintain her needs while traveling. There are many wicked minded and evil men around the world who are

---

[95] "Mahram" is a male-relative of a woman who can see her in private, stay and travel with her, due to marital relation, if he is a husband, a father in-law, or a son in-law, or he is blood related to her and cannot marry her such as a father, a son, an uncle from either side, a grandfather from both sides, or a grandson or a nephew.

[96] This Hadith is reported by Bukhari and Muslim.

willing to take advantage of a weak woman who is alone or traveling alone. Such wicked-minded men are either interested in the wealth of a single woman, her body and physical attractions, or both. A woman is an easy target for wicked-minded men and an easy victim as well due to her physical and emotional make-up. A woman is in need for a man to help her secure all her needs, take care of her and provide all needed care, security and attention in order not to become in need of a stranger, who might very well take advantage of her needs. A 'Mahram' of a woman in Islam will fulfill all the needs of a woman, gladly and with a smile on his face, as this is a rewarded duty by Allah (ﷻ).

A Mahram therefore is like a sincere, honest, fully paid servant for a woman, at no extra charge to her. He is also a protector, a caretaker and a companion who will provide her with maximum care, protection and service. A Mahram will also provide a protecting shield for a woman against wicked minded and evil people who would like to take advantage of a single woman at any cost.

Who would think, after all, forbidding a woman to travel alone is a humiliating factor and an insult to her honor, dignity, pride and intelligence? It is, in fact, an honor to find a willing man to serve, protect and give decent moral and meaningful companionship to a traveling woman, free of charge.

Women's Beating

Allah (ﷻ), stated in the Glorious Quran 4:34 which the meaning of is translated as:

"...As to those women on whose part you see ill-conduct, admonish them (first), (next), refuse to share their beds, (and last) beat them (lightly, if it is useful), but if they return to obedience, seek not against them means (of annoyance). Surely, Allah is Most High, Most Great."

Islam, in fact, forbids beating women and warns strictly against it. This is due to the general basic fact that women, in general, are physically weaker than men in their physical make-up are. Women are usually unable to defend themselves against beating. However, although beating of women is forbidden, Islam permitted it in restricted and very limited occasions and only when it is required as a final treatment of a persistent situation, i.e. when a wife disobeys her husband's instructions for no visible and acceptable valid reason.

In the verse we quoted from the Glorious Quran, Allah (ﷻ) dealt with the case of a wife who disobeys her husband's commands and instructions. The treatment of this extremely sensitive issue comes on gradual stages, as we have noticed from the verse. Medicine, or treatment of any ailment, can be very bitter at times. But an ill person will take the remedy gladly and bear the bitterness of the medicine in order to be cured from his illness. The remedy to treat a disobedient wife, as we have noticed, comes on three gradual stages, as illustrated by Allah (ﷻ) in the Glorious Quran.

First stage: The stage of advice, counseling and warning against Allah's penalty. A husband must remind his disobedient wife with the importance of following the instructions of the husband in Islam. This stage is a very kind and easy one. But, if this treatment does not work and prove not effective, then comes the next stage.

Second stage: To leave the wife's bed. Or, if one sleeps in the same bed with her, he will turn his back to her, not touch her, talk to her and have intercourse with her. This stage, as noticed, combines both strictness and kindness, although it is a very harsh practice on both. But, if this treatment does not work, then turn to the final stage of discipline below.

Third and final stage: Beating without hurting, breaking a bone, leaving blue or black marks on the body and avoiding hitting the face, at any cost. The purpose of beating here is a disciplinary action and not retaliation or hurting by any means. It is to let the wife know that her behavior, conduct and attitude towards her husband are not acceptable. Beating, in this case, and according to Islamic teachings, is restricted and limited to be a form of treatment only. Beating a wife is not meant to be a form of humiliation, a form of forcing and compelling the woman to do things against her own will, or a means of hurting her physically. In fact, it is reported that Ibn 'Abbas (﷽), one of the leading companions of the Prophet (ﷺ) and a scholar of early Muslims, hit only with the (Siwak) the natural wooden root that is used for brushing the teeth. Islam forbids severe beating as punishment.

This treatment is proved to be very effective with two types of women, as psychologists have determined:

The first type: Controlling or mastering women. These are the type of women who like to control, master and run the affairs of their husbands by pushing them around, commanding them and give them orders.

The second type: Submissive, or subdued women. These women enjoy being beaten. G. A. Holdfield, a European psychologist, in his book *Psychology and Morals* states the following:

"The instinct of submission strengthen at times, in the human being so much that a submissive person will enjoy seeing someone overpowering him, over-ruling him and being cruel to him. Such a submissive person bears the consequences of his submission due to the fact that he enjoys the pain. This is a well spread instinct amongst women even if they do not realize it. For this very reason, women are well known being more forbearing to pain than men. A wife of this type of women becomes more attracted to and admiring of her husband when he beats her. Nothing, on the other hand, will sadden some women, such as, much as a soft, very kind and very obedient husband who is never upset regardless of being challenged!"

Beating, in according to the Islamic teachings, is listed as the last and final stage of training, discipline and upbringing methods. Islam does not permit, allow or even condone beating unless the first two stages are proven to be ineffective methods of treatment. Moreover, beating must not be employed as a remedy if a wife prefers to be divorced.

Again, the beating of a wife must be in strict privacy. A wife must not be beaten before her children or any one else for that matter. Beating is considered a means of discipline and right upbringing. A father, for instance, may spank his child for doing something wrong. A teacher will also spank a student for doing something wrong, such as neglecting a homework, being late or tardy to class or school, cheating on the test, talking back to the teacher and so on. Striking here is a means of upbringing and discipline. That is why Allah (ﷻ) illustrated at the end of the verse that deals with beating the disobedient wife that:

"But if they return to obedience, seek not against them means [of annoyance]...." Glorious Quran 4:34 which the meaning of is translated as.

This assures that the three stages of discipline stated in the Glorious Quran are meant only for a good disciplining cause. Islam does not aim to destroy the family and causing it to become burdened with unnecessary pain, headache and problems. The true destruction of a family is when the wife becomes a victim of divorce.

In a recent statistics in Britain[97], it was declared that the number of wives whom have been brutally beaten by their husbands has risen from 6,400 in 1990 to 30,000 in 1992. This number jumped to 65,400 women in 1995. Statisticians expect this number to double 124,400 towards the end of the twentieth century! These statistics, as the report says, were based on information gathered

---

[97] *Al-Usrah [Family] Magazine*, Jumada I, 1416 H.

from police department. But, what about the unreported cases of wife-beating, and women in general, which are not reported!

Mrs. Anni Besant stated[98], while comparing between Islamic Laws and Western legislation insofar as women's rights are concerned:

"Islamic Laws are among the best laws known to the world, insofar as woman is concerned. It is the most fair and just legislation. It exceeds the Western legislation concerning real estate, inheritance and divorce laws. It acts as a guardian for women's rights. Phrases such as "One Wife is Sufficient for a man", and "Polygamy", mystified people and deviated them away from the real misery which Western women suffer and live. Many husbands left their wives after they have got what they wanted from them. In fact such men show no care, concern or mercy for their wives."

---

[98] *The Life and Teachings of Mohammed Madras,* 1932.

Conclusion

Islam is the eternal divine message of Allah (ﷻ) to all men delivered by Allah's Prophet (ﷺ). A group of mankind believed in the Message of Islam and followed it, while others disbelieved in it. The Message of Islam declared at the beginning of the revelation that the human being is dignified and honored more than all other creatures.

Allah (ﷻ), stated in the Glorious Quran 17:70 which the meaning of is translated as:

"And indeed We have honored the children of Adam, and We have carried them on land and sea, and have provided them with lawful good things, and have preferred them above many of those whom We have created with a marked preference."

Allah (ﷻ) also declared another major principle of man's life on Earth, after the first principle was declared.

"All men are created equal in terms of original creation."

Allah (ﷻ) stated in the Glorious Quran 4:1 which the meaning of is translated as:

"O mankind! Be dutiful to Your Lord, Who created you from a single person (Adam), and from him (Adam) He created many men and women and fear Allah through Whom you demand

your mutual (rights), and (do not cut the relations of) the wombs (kinship). Surely, Allah is Ever an All Watcher over you."

Based on the previous principles, all men are equal in terms of human values. All men and women are equal in terms of expressing their opinion and utilizing all that has been established on Earth for them by Their Creator, Allah (ﷻ). All men and women are created equal in the sight of Allah. If there are differences between the various members of mankind, it is truly not on the basis of honor and lineage. If there are different levels of people in terms of living standards, income, etc., this does not reflect, by any means, a difference in the human nature of these classes of people. Distinction between the levels of mankind is based on their true commitment to Islam and their level of practice and application of its principles in their own lives. Allah (ﷻ), stated this principle in the Glorious Quran 49:13 which the meaning of is translated as:

"O Mankind! We have created you from a male and a female, and made you into nations and tribes, that you may know one another. Verily, the most honorable of you in the Sight of Allah is that who is most pious and righteous. Verily, Allah is All-Knowing, All-Aware."

Honoring a person, in the Sight of Allah is not on the basis of color, social status, sex, race, strength, health, dignity or wealth. All men are created equal. The only measure of distinction and differentiation in the Sight of Allah (ﷻ) is strictly on the basis of piety and performance of good deeds.

Similarly, Allah's Prophet (ﷺ) was also reported as saying:

"An Arab has no virtue over a non-Arab. A white has no virtue over a black except with the amount of piety." [99]

Islamic teachings remove all differences between men and places them all on equal footing. One of the essential and integral teachings of Islam, which is really misunderstood, misconstrued and not well explained, is that "a female is equal to a male in everything except where there is a clear and distinct call for exception". These exceptions were the subject of our booklet. We have attempted to clarify all these misconceptions about women that many people have, including Arabs, Muslims and non-Muslims, about the reality of Islam.

Allah (ﷺ), stated in the Glorious Quran 9:71 which the meaning of is translated as:

"The believers, men and women, are helpers, supporters, friends and protectors of one another; they enjoin (on the people) Islamic Monotheism and that Islam orders one to do, and forbid (people) from all forms of evil (i.e. polytheism of all kinds, and all that Islam has forbidden; they offer their prayers perfectly, and give their charity and obey Allah and His Messenger. Allah will shower His Mercy upon them. Surely Allah is All-Mighty, All-Wise."

Allah (ﷺ), stated in the Glorious Quran 3:195 which the meaning of is translated as:

---

[99] This Hadith was reported by Ahmad.

*"So their Lord accepted (their supplication and answered them),
"Never will I allow to be lost the work of any one of you, be he
male or female. You are (members) one of another..."*

Allah (ﷻ), stated in the Glorious Quran 4:7 which the meaning
of is translated as:

*"There is a share for men and a share for women from what is
left by parents and those closely related, whether, the property
be small or large, a legal share."*

Based upon what has been said and elaborated upon in this entire
booklet, one can comfortably and confidently say that women
never have, and will never ever enjoy full rights, natural freedom
and complete personal rights except in the SHADE of ISLAM.
Islam has established and set forth a set of rights for women. It
sets and names certain duties that she must maintain, be
committed to and perform. All this is due to the fact that Islam is
a divine religion, as opposed to man-made laws. It is for the
entire mankind, male and female, rich and poor, king and
peasant, healthy and ill, rich and poor, strong and weak, white,
black, red or yellow. They are all alike and equal in the Sight of
Their Creator, Allah (ﷻ). Allah, the Creator, knows best what
benefits and improves the situations of all His creation both in
this world and in the hereafter.

I would like to request the reader not to pass judgment on Islam
on the basis of what he/she may see, observe or notice in the
behavior, attitude and bad-practices of a group of Muslim

individuals who claim close ties to Islam. In fact, there are some people who use Islam as a blanket to cover up their personal crimes, sins and shameful deeds. Similarly, there are many individuals who are counted as Muslims, as they declare by their lips and tongues that "There is no deity worthy of worship but Allah Alone, and Mohammad (ﷺ) is the slave servant, and Messenger of Allah (ﷺ)". However, these individuals stop at this point only and do not perform their Islamic duties, practice their commitment to Islam in terms of the good morals that Islam calls for. They may lie, deceive, cheat, and commit various kinds of sins and crimes, which are neither condoned nor accepted by Islam, of which they claim to be a part.

Islam is a wholesome religion. It is so vast, yet simple to apply. There are individuals who strive throughout their entire lifetime to be good Muslims, to attain the best and most perfect level of practice, seeking the pleasure of Allah (ﷺ), in all that they do. On the other hand, there are individuals who have shortcomings, commissions and omissions which they deserve to be punished for in this world and in the hereafter. However, no one can accuse such sinners and label them "condemned and outside the fold of Islam, because of the sins they have committed." Such individuals are called, in accordance with Islamic teachings and terminology ""Asee", a sinning disobedient person who is neglecting the commands of Allah (ﷺ), the instructions and beautiful teachings of Allah's Prophet (ﷺ) and the general Islamic teachings.

It is understood that "lacking something, such as wealth, happiness or morals, will not enable the lacking person to share with others what he does not own." This principle applies to Islam as well.

For those who are keen to learn more about Islam, our advice to them is to seek knowledge from those who are well-known for their knowledge, understanding and practice of Islam onto their own lives. Our advice is "not to ask a non-practicing Muslim anything about Islam." Such a person, definitely, will mislead you.

Surface knowledge of Islam is also very dangerous, harmful and detrimental. Reading a few books about Islam, regardless of whether they are reliable sources or not, will not qualify a person to pass verdicts and disseminate sound knowledge about Islam and its practices. Following the opinions of others blindly is also very dangerous and harmful. It is compulsory to seek unbiased opinions about Islam.

Finally, I request every non-Muslim with a sound mind and heart to read a bit of information about Islam from reliable sources that are knowledgeable, God-fearing and well known as honest Muslim writers. It is good and beneficial knowledge to those who do not know anything about Islam. For those who already know something about Islam, it can only increase their knowledge and Islamic education. Allah (ﷻ), stated in the Glorious Quran 2:256 which the meaning of is translated as:
"There is no compulsion in religion. Verily, the Right Path has become distinct from the wrong path. Whoever disbelieves in the 'Taghut' (anything worshipped other than Allah and believes in Allah, then he has grasped the trustworthiest handhold that will never break. Allah is the All-Hearer, All-Knowing."

***

ISLAMIC BROTHERHOOD

On the authority of Abu Huraira رضي الله عنه who said: The Messenger of Allah صلى الله عليه وسلم said:

Do not envy one another; do not inflate prices one to another; do not hate one another; do not turn away from one another; and do not uundercut one another, but be you, O slaves of Allah, brothers. A Muslim is the brother of a Muslim: he neither oppresses him nor disgraces him, he neither lies to him not does he hold him in contempt. Piety and righteousness is here - and he pointed to his breast three times. It is evil enough for a man to hold his brother Muslim in contempt. The whole of a Muslim for another Muslim is inviolable: his blood, his property, and his honour.

It was related by Muslim.

If you have any inquiry please contact one of the following addresses

Germany:
1- Tarag ibn Zyed germany - Frankfort - Tel: 06997390353 Or 06997390354 - Fax: 06997390355
2- Kreis Isamischer Shudenten Heidelberg - Leimerstr 50 69126 Heidelberg Germany - Tel: 006221/768236 order 451635 - fax: 06221/768064 order 763424

United Kingdom:
1- Markazi Jamiat Ahl-e-Hadith U.K - 20 Green Lane, small Heath, Birmingham B9 5DB - Tel: 0121 773 0019 Fax: 0121 766 8779
2- Banbury Islamic Centre - 55 park Road, Banbury, Oxon Ox16 - Tel/Fax: 01295 264078
3- Muhammadi Masjid & Madrasah Salafia - 24 - 36 Hartopp Road, Alum Rock, Bermingham B8 - Tel: 0121 328 7773
4- Mosque & Islamic School - 29 Queens Cross, Dudley DY11Qn - Tel: 01384 258479
5- Muhammadi Mosque & Islamc Centre 5 Camden Terrace, Bradford BD8 7HX - Tel: 01274 728993
6- Masjid & Madrasah al - Farooq - 32 - 38 Dixon Avenue, Crosshill, Glasgow G42 8EJ - Tel: 0141 433 2686 Fax: 0141 453 0422
7- Masjid at - Taqwa -1 Harewood Street. Leicester LE53LX -Tel: 01162126772
8- Jamia Masjid Ahl-e-0Hadith - 97 Hopwood Lane, Halifax, HX1 4ET - Tel: 01422356843

Finland:
Islamic Cultural Community Of Finland & Helsinki Islam Center - P.O. Box 33700100 Helsinki. Finland
Tel: 003589736899
Fax: 003589735512

Saudi Arabia:
1- cooperative office for call and Guidance in Al-Bat'ha area (Riyadh)
Tel: 00966 - 1 - 4030251
Fax: 00966 - 1 - 4059387
P.O.Box: 20824 Riyadh 11465
www.cocg.org
2- Cooperative office for call and Guidance in Sultanah area (Riyadh) - Tel: 00966 - 1 - 4240077 - Fax: 00966 - 1 - 4251005 - P.O.Box: 92675 Riyadh 11663
3- Cooperative office for call and Guidance in Alraboha area (Riyadh) - Tel: 00966- 1 - 4916065 - Fax: 00966-1- 4970126
4- Cooperative office for call and Guidance in Jeddah - Tel: 00966-2-6829898 Fax: 00966-2-6829898 - P.O.Box: 6897 Jeddah 21452
5- Cooperative office for call and Guidance in Alkobar - Tel: 00966-3-8987444 - Fax: 00966-3-8987444 - P.O.Box: 31131 Dammam
6- Cooperative office for call and Guidance in Jubail - Tel: 00966-3-3613626 Fax: 00966-3-3611234

U. S. A:

1- Islamic Society Of Bravard County 550 Florida ave - Melbourne, Fl 32901 U.S.A - Phone (407) 726-9357
2- 8500 Hilltop Road Fairfax, Virginia 22031 - Tel: (703) 641-4890 (703) 641-4891 - Fax: (703) 641 - 4899
www.iiasa. org
Email - info@iiasa.org
3- The Islamic Center Of Charlotte (ICC) 1700 Progress Lane Charlotte, NC 28205 - Phone # (704) 537-9399 - Fax: # (704) 537 - 1577
4- Al Qur'aan was - Sunnah Society of Na - 19800 Vandyke Rd - Detriot, MI 48234 - Tel: (313) 893 - 3767, Fax: (313) 893-3748
email: Quransunna @aol.com

Sweden:

1- Islamiska Sunni Centert Goteborg Sweden General sgatan 2- A - 4150 Goteborg
Tel: 004631843917
Fax: 004631843917
Mobile: 0046703353617
2- Islamiska Kultur Foreningen I Malmo.
Box: 18003 20032 Malmo - SwedenTel:004640948839
Fax: 004640944189
Or 004640211703

Japan:

1- 40 - 13 HIRAOKA - Cho HACHIOJI - shi, TOKYO 192 - 0061 - JAPAN
TAWHID MOSQ
2- Japan - Islamic center
1- 16 - 11 Ohara - Setagaya - ku Tokyo - 156 - 0041
Tel: 03- 3460 - 6169
Fax: 03 - 3460 - 6105

France:

1- Assoctation chemin Droit 81 Rue Rochechouart 75009 - Paris -France Tel:01-48221986 (0033148221986)
Fax:01-48221049 (003148221049)

Danemark:

1- det islamiske Trossam find pa fyn. Odense- Danmark
Qrbakvej 247.5220 Odenes
Tel: 004566106608
Fax: 004566159117
2- Den lighed & brabreskabfare { Arhus Branbrand } Danmark
Grimbojvej 15.8220 Brabrand Aarhus - Denmark
Tel: 0045867552611
Or 004586755161 -
Fax: 004586755261
Or 004586261713

Belgium:

1- Center d Education et Gulturel de Jeunesss Section foundation Al haramain Belgigue - 100,Rue de la limite. 1210 Bruzelles - Tel: 003222237890
Fax: 003222237890

Hollande:

1- Stichting El twheed Dellamystraat 49hs. 1053 BG Amsterdam Holland
Tel: 0031235311816
Fax: 0031235311816

SOME USEFUL ISLAMIC WEB.SITES

- www.beconvinced.com
- www.islamtoday.com
- www.islam-guide.com
- www.al-sunnah.com
- www.thetruereligion.org
- www.it-is-truth.org
- www.islam-qa.com
- www.plaintruth.org
- www.islamunveiled.com
- www.prophetmuhammed.org
- www.alharamain.org
- www.sultan.org
- www.islamworld.net
- www.islamland.org

المرأة
في ظلال الإسلام